Your House
in
Needlepoint

Your House
in
Needlepoint

Susan Higginson

COLLINS & BROWN

First published in Great Britain in 1990 by
Collins & Brown Limited
Mercury House, 195 Knightsbridge
London SW7 1RE

ISBN 1 85585 045 1

A CIP catalogue record for this book
is available from the British Library

Designed and produced by
Alphabet & Image Ltd
Sherborne, Dorset.

Typeset by Susan Higginson
Printed in Hong Kong by Regent Publishing Services Ltd

Acknowledgements

I should like to thank my family and friends for their interest
and encouragement during the production of this book.
Thanks also to my former students who generously allowed
me to use their work as illustrations, Anne Clarke (Modern
Bungalow), Nancy Llewellyn (Farmhouse), Heather Prescott
(Victorian House) and Yvonne Robinson (Cottage in Sepia
tones).
This book is dedicated to Derek, Cathy and Lizzie.
All at Alphabet & Image constantly helped, encouraged and
came up with all sorts of good ideas. Their assistance was
invaluable.
The watercolour on page 74 is by Martha Gumn, courtesy
BAS Printers, Stockbridge. All diagrams by the author.

Contents

Needlepoint houses illustrated

Introduction

Many people, having worked several needlepoint kits, feel that they would like to be more adventurous and design a piece of work for themselves. Immediately, however, the next thoughts are, 'I'm not artistic enough,' 'I haven't enough imagination,' or 'It's far too complicated.'

For a first attempt at designing therefore, it is a good idea to take as your subject something in which the basic design features are already laid down, and all you have to do is to transfer them on to the canvas. What better subject than your own house, or that of a friend or relative?

Houses as subjects have a distinct advantage when it comes to working with the square canvas mesh, in that they are constructed on a geometric grid, with vertical walls, rectangular windows and doors, upright chimneys and horizontal steps, all of which are easily depicted on the canvas. Another advantage of working a design of a house you are familiar with is that you can take any number of helpful photographs of it, and can, in any moment of uncertainty, pop out and have a look at it.

In this book I have tried to provide answers to the numerous questions which come up in a project such as this, from the order of working to the best stitches to use for a variety of effects. There are also many illustrations of different types of houses, which should prove helpful in the designing of your own picture.

Perhaps the most important reason for choosing to work a needlepoint picture of your own home is that it is a very satisfying thing to do and a really delightful thing to have, especially treasured when eventually you move house.

1 Materials and Techniques

Unlike many craft activities, the equipment necessary for needlepoint (also called canvas work or tapestry) is very simple and relatively inexpensive. The costliest piece of equipment you might buy is a frame of some sort, and with a little ingenuity a perfectly adequate one can be put together by a complete amateur, as will be shown later in the chapter. Since there is so little to buy, it is certainly worth purchasing the best materials available, as a needlepoint picture, particularly of a house you have lived in, will be a much valued object, and it would be a pity if the materials were not worthy of all the hard work and attention lavished on it.

Canvas

Canvas for needlepoint varies in its colour, type of mesh and finish, so it can be rather bewildering for a beginner to know which is the most appropriate for the purpose.

Colour is largely a matter of choice, though of course it is much easier to trace a picture on to a canvas overlay if the canvas is white rather than dull brown. I always use white canvas and find that in artificial light it is easier to see the mesh, but I know that to many people it is rather bright. The most usual colours other than white are ecru and brown. Interlock canvas is usually white.

There are two types of mesh, single (or mono) and double (or Penelope). Double mesh is only used if the article to be made will receive so much wear that an extra (tramming) thread needs to be laid down along the double mesh and under the stitching to give additional strength. This is unlikely to be the case with a picture of a house, and single mesh canvas is

the best type to choose for work of this nature.

Within the single mesh category there is another division, between interwoven and interlock canvases. Interwoven has a warp and weft woven in the normal way, whereas with interlock canvases, the warp or vertical threads divide round the weft threads to lock them in position, thus ensuring that edges do not fray when cut, and even when the canvas has been handled and perhaps lost its stiffness, the threads do not move and distort the size and shape of the original squares. If you are using a frame, which will keep the canvas taut at all times, it does not really matter whether you choose interwoven or interlock canvas, but if you are working without a frame and the canvas will be rolled or even folded when you are not actually stitching, and possibly scrunched up when you are, it is much better to choose interlock canvas, which will hold its shape better. Do however make sure that whichever canvas you choose is made of high quality materials, some cheaper canvases are made stiff with a great deal of sizing instead of being woven with good quality cotton, so look around and compare before you buy.

Canvas mesh varies from large squares of three threads to the inch (2.5cm) to tiny squares of more than twenty threads to the inch. Which you choose will depend on how much detail you want in your work, and how much time you are prepared to spend on any given project. If you are making a carpet or large wall-hanging you would be unlikely to choose a small mesh canvas as a lot of detail is probably unnecessary. On the other hand if you are working a miniature you would choose the smallest canvas you could comfortably work with, as otherwise you would be unable to put any detail in at all and the end result would be disappointing.

For a needlepoint picture worked in crewel wools, a 13s or 14s single mesh canvas, that is one with 13 or 14 threads to the inch (2.5cm), is probably best, as this will comfortably accommodate three strands of wool in the needle for the stitching, thus giving opportunities for subtle shading of colours.

If you are working a small or miniature picture and perhaps using stranded cottons, choose a single mesh canvas with 18 threads to the inch (2.5cm) which can be used with the full six

Country House – stitches used:

Sky: Milanese stitch in various blues, pale greys and white. The clouds are also Milanese stitch and the whole was worked in the patchy colour technique explained in Chapter 3.

Roof: Five different shades are used in this brick stitch roof. Notice the intentional break in the pattern where the extension joins the main house. The Parisian stitch was worked up to the end of the house, with compensation stitches put in where necessary, and then the extension was worked as a separate piece of stitchery.

Chimneys: Parisian stitch.

Walls: The walls are in Parisian stitch worked sideways. Five different colours of wool are mixed in the needle (three at a time), to give a natural look to the stone.

Window frames: Worked in tent stitch, as are the glazing bars. It is not easy to show any difference in thickness between the frames and the bars on a picture of this size.

Windows: Diagonal satin stitch worked in iron grey, black or a mixture of the two. Some windows have a strand of paler grey to simulate reflections in the glass. Curtains are shown at a few windows by straight stitches at various angles.

Door: Diagonal satin stitch over two canvas threads worked in different directions.

Drainpipe and guttering: Back stitch as a surface stitch to emphasise the three-dimensional nature of the features.

Bushes (left to right): French knots, bullion, detached chain, fly, detached chain, straight stitches, horizontal stitches with French knots, fly, random straight stitches and French knots on stalks.

Creeper: French knots and straight stitches.

Tree on left: The leaves are fan stitches with many slight variations of shape.

Hedge on right: Single trammed Gobelin with added French knots.

Gravel: Hungarian stitch.

Country House

A country house built in honey-coloured stone with a rosy tiled roof. The colours of the more recent extension on the right are slightly different so that this feature is seen to be set back from the main house. This is also emphasised by the break in the Parisian stitch pattern. This picture is a good example of the extensive use of colour mixing in the needle. In nearly all the features more than one shade is used in the needle at any one time, and this certainly results in the finished picture looking very natural. There is extensive use of surface stitchery, adding a realistic three-dimensional look to the house and its surroundings. This picture is worked in wools on 13s interlock canvas.

strands of cotton, in any colour mixtures required.

When working with a large piece of canvas it is preferable to have the selvage at the side of the work, as you would with any material; if, however, you are working a tiny miniature, this is unimportant.

Any type of canvas can be painted, either to help you see the shape of your design, or perhaps to hide any canvas threads which might show through when straight stitches are being used in the design. In this case, it is a good idea to add an extra strand of thread, so that coverage is better. If you want to paint your canvas, use dryish acrylic paints which will not run if you dampen the canvas later on in the stretching process. Be careful when painting that you do not get the canvas wet as it will lose its stiffness.

Threads

Many different threads are sold for needlepoint and others may be used which are not specifically made for use with canvas, such as knitting wools and metallic threads. However, the most suitable threads if you are working a picture of a house are crewel wools or 6-strand mercerised cotton embroidery floss. The great advantage of crewel wool is that it is fine and is manufactured in a very extensive range of colours, with shadings of each colour. This means that it is possible to mix two or even three shades of wool together in the needle to achieve the exact colouring required. This is also possible with the 6-strand embroidery floss, where the strands may be separated and different colours put together in the needle. The mercerised cotton threads do not mix quite as well as the crewel wools since the colours are, on the whole, less subtle, but nevertheless mixing colours in the needle makes such a difference to the look of the finished work that it should be done whenever possible.

Other wools which are produced for needlepoint are Persian yarn and Tapisserie wool. Persian yarn consists of three strands of 2-ply wool plied loosely together, but colours cannot be mixed in the needle to any great extent as the basic 2-ply thread is too thick. It is, however, of high quality and can be used

satisfactorily in single colour work. Tapisserie wool can only be used with 10 thread to the inch (2.5cm) canvas as it cannot be divided at all and as such its uses are limited. Perle cotton is made in two thicknesses and can be useful to give a shiny contrast on a wool background. Soft embroidery cotton has a matt finish and is best used on its own for pictures entirely worked in straight stitch, as it has a rather stringy texture which does not mix very well with other threads. All of these threads have large colour ranges.

Needles

Blunt-ended tapestry needles should always be used, as otherwise it is possible that the point of the needle may go through the canvas thread instead of the hole, with disastrous results. Tapestry needles are available in either mixed packs or packets of six of the same size. The correct size for 12s, 13s and 14s canvas mesh is 20, and for 18s canvas you should use a size 22. To check whether your needle is correct for the canvas you are using, drop the needle diagonally into one of the holes. If it is the correct size it should just rest without falling through, but should not distort the mesh when pulled through to the back of the canvas.

Frames

When working on a piece of needlepoint of any size and importance, it is advisable to have the work on a frame. This will not only make the stitching easier, but will also help to avoid distorting the shape of the finished picture. Many types of frame are now available, some floor-standing, others hand-held, so make sure you buy one that is comfortable to hold or to sit at and has the following three essential features. Firstly it should be wide enough for you to attach the whole width of your canvas across it without turning any in; secondly, you should be able to roll your work round the top and bottom of the frame to expose different parts of your work without taking the frame apart, and thirdly, when the work is in position you must be able to tighten up the bars of the frame so that the canvas is held taught.

A simple but quite adequate frame can be made from two pieces of 0.75 inch (2cm) dowel rod, two pieces of flat wooden bar 0.75 inch (2cm) wide and 0.25 inch (0.75cm) thick, and four butterfly nuts with matching screw-threaded rod (studding) 1.75 inches (4.5cm) long.

Method of construction:
1. Decide how big you want the frame. I have one which measures 17 inches by 12.5 inches (43cm x 32cm) which I find very versatile.
2. Cut two pieces of dowel the length of the longer sides. Cut two pieces of flat wooden bar the length of the shorter sides. Glass paper the ends to remove any burrs.
3. Drill holes in the ends of the dowels to accommodate the studding to a depth of about one inch (2.5cm). Leave 0.75 inch (2cm) sticking out at the ends. Make sure the studding is firmly bedded in by using a strong glue.
4. Drill holes in each end of the two bars, about 0.5 inch (1.5cm) from the end, large enough for the studding.
5. Attach a piece of heading tape (as used in curtain making) to each dowel, either with a staple gun or small nails or tacks. The canvas can be sewn to this if you do not want to staple it to the dowel with a staple gun.
6. Assemble the frame by putting the flat sides against the ends of the dowels, with the studding sticking out through the holes. Tighten up with butterfly nuts.

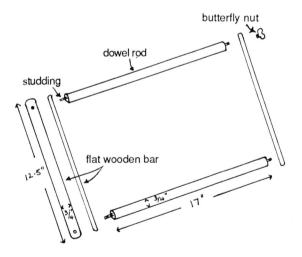

Making your own frame

Other useful items

You will need a large pair of scissors for cutting canvas and a small pair of pointed embroidery scissors for use while working. An HB pencil and a rubber if necessary are used for transferring designs on to the canvas, while a dark, fairly thick fibre-tipped pen is useful for going over the lines of your initial drawing on paper. Never draw on the canvas with anything very dark as it is surprising how easily these lines show through pale-coloured threads.

Basic techniques

Although everybody develops his or her own favourite techniques for any craft activity, there are nevertheless various basic points worth considering which, if followed, will enhance the look of the finished product.

Length of thread: The constant movement of the thread backwards and forwards through the canvas wears the thread quickly, and it is sensible therefore to limit the length of each piece of thread to about twenty inches (50cms), or shorter if the stitch being used is very small.

Threading the needle: If you have difficulties with this, and many people do, try using a commercial needle threader, or the following method. Pinch the folded wool over the eye end of the needle and slide off while holding the fold of wool tightly. You should then be able to push the eye of the needle down on to this fold and pull the fold through the eye.

Making the stitches: To start a new piece of thread after some work has been done, the best method is to run the needle and thread through the stitchery already on the canvas for about 0.75 inch (2cm). Do not pull the first stitch too tightly as this might pull the end right out. When starting on a bare canvas, hold about 0.75 inch (2cm) of thread along the back of the work in the direction you are working, and stitch over it. To finish off a length of thread, take it through to the back of the work and run it through about 0.75 inch (2cm) of worked stitchery. Cut all loose ends of thread off flush with the back of the work, as otherwise these may be pulled through to the front when making another stitch. When making needlepoint stitches, with a few exceptions, stab

1920s Semi-detached House – stitches used:

Sky: Milanese stitch.

Roof: Single brick stitch in a mixture of grey and wine-red. Single straight stitches were placed along the top and sloping side of the roof and then crossed with small stitches at intervals to give a ridged effect.

Chimney: Single brick stitch in grey with a single brick stitch top matching the gable. Black chimney pots.

Gable: Outlined with a single diagonal stitch each side. Small stitches were then placed over these long stitches at intervals to give a ridged effect to the gable.

House walls: Arrowhead stitch worked sideways in white.

Window frames: Tent stitch, as are the glazing bars.

Windows: Diagonal satin stitch worked in black.

Door: The top of the door is worked as a window, while the lower section has two panels of diagonal satin stitch over two canvas threads, worked between three lines of tent stitch.

Drainpipe: The drainpipe is a single strand of cotton taken down the full height of the house on top of the arrowhead stitch of the wall.

Hedge: Hungarian stitch in a mixture of two colours of green. No compensation stitches were put in, so the top of the stitchery is uneven, thus looking like an undulating hedge.

Path: Brick stitch.

Fence: Lines of vertical tent stitch, with two straight stitches along the top.

Foreground: Double brick stitch.

Tree, bushes and grass: The tree is straight stitches and French knots, the flowers by the front door are also French knots and the grass is single brick stitch.

1920s Semi-detached House

Very many of these houses were built in England in the 1920s and 1930s, and even though the design is simple, a needlepoint picture can look very attractive, especially if the shape of the large bay windows can be suggested. In the present case this was achieved by working first, in single brick stitch, the centre panel between the upper and lower bay windows, in a mixture of wine red and black. Then, with a darker mixture of threads, the side panels were worked so that the stitches did not quite match up with the centre panel, thus creating definite breaks in the stitchery to mark the angles of the bay. Although an attempt could be made to suggest the many small panes of the original windows in surface stitchery, it was thought that this might look rather fussy and spoil the general effect. This picture is worked in 6-strand embroidery floss on 18s interlock canvas.

stitch should be used, that is, the needle and thread should be pushed straight through the canvas to the full extent of the thread, and then back in a similar fashion. This way an even tension is maintained and there is minimum wear on the thread.

Compensation stitches: There are many different-sized stitches in needlepoint, and it is this variety which makes it possible to design interesting and three-dimensional pieces of work. However, the use of large stitches and uneven outlines does result in there being many occasions when a whole stitch will not fit in the available space. You then have to work what is known as a compensation stitch.This is done by working as much of the main stitch as is possible in the space, being careful to take the thread across the canvas at the same angle as the original stitch. When working a row of stitches which needs to start with one or more compensation stitches it is often difficult to work out which canvas threads these first few stitches should cover. In this case, it is best to work a whole stitch which can easily be placed correctly in relation to other whole stitches further down the row, and then go back to insert the compensation stitches before continuing.

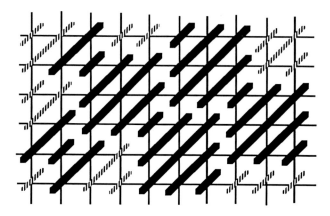

The dashed lines are the compensation stitches necessary in this rectangle of diagonal ground stitch.

2 Designing the Picture

Ideally, in order to work a picture of your house in needlepoint you need a picture of the house taken from the required viewpoint. To make full use of the square mesh of the canvas, it is best, certainly for a first attempt, to work your design of the front or back of your house from a straight viewpoint. Although perspective views look very attractive on a photograph, it is difficult to make them look as good on canvas because the stitches cannot easily be made to fit neatly into the odd shaped areas of the drawing, and the many straight stitches which are so useful for architecture cannot be used satisfactorily. Sometimes it is not possible to get a photograph from the required viewpoint because trees, bushes, hedges or other buildings obscure the view. In these cases either make a suitable drawing, which need only be very simple, or take several photographs from inside the barrier showing overlapping sections of the house. These may later be used together in making a master drawing, and although taking the photograph from close up probably makes the house look very distorted, any photographs are better than none, and actual measurements can be checked against the real house. If you look at the finished needlepoint houses in this book, you will see in some cases how a less than ideal photograph has been adapted in this way.

The next step is to decide how large you want your whole picture to be, and how big the house should be within that picture. The ideal completed size will depend on what you want to do with the finished work — frame it, make it into a cushion or even hang it as a tapestry. The house, as the subject of the picture, should generally take up a fairly large proportion of the whole, but needs to be placed firmly in its setting if it is to look really effective. Of course, if the garden is a major feature of the property, then more prominence should be placed upon it. Do avoid a close-up view of the house placed right in the middle of the picture with very little around it.

Having decided how big the house should be, this idea must then be compared with the working photos or drawings to see whether these need to be enlarged or reduced to make them suitable as models.

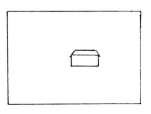

Only a good idea if the surroundings are as important as the house. (see Australian Outback picture.)

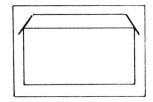

Too little space around the house.

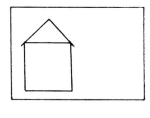

The house is too far to one side, unless another important feature is to fill the rest of the picture. A semi-detached house may look best against one edge of the picture, but do not have a very large area on the other side.

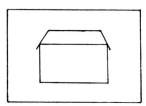

The house is absolutely central, making the design rather boring.

Positioning the house in the picture

Modern Bungalow – stitches used:

Sky: Chevron stitch in a mixture of blues and white.
Roof: Small Parisian stitch worked sideways.
House walls: Double brick stitch worked sideways.
Window frames: Tent stitch.
Windows: Diagonal satin stitch.
Door: Cross stitch.
Tree on left: Leaf stitch.
Fencing: Double brick stitch.
Trellis on wall: Single trammed Gobelin.
Tree in foreground: Byzantine stitch.
Paving: Hungarian diamonds.
Grass: Hungarian stitch.
Flowers: French knots, spider's webs.

Modern Bungalow

A small modern house such as this may not at first seem to have much character as a subject, especially as the garden is newly planted, but a former student of the author, to whom it belongs, has managed to make it interesting by clever choice of stitches and good colour mixing. The sky in chevron stitch is especially noteworthy for its subtle colour graduations. A degree of artistic licence has been used in making the garden much more luxuriant than it appears on the colour print and the house next door has been omitted. Although the bungalow is placed dead centre in the picture, this looks all right because the house itself is not symmetrical, having a gable at its right-hand end. This picture is worked in crewel wools on interlock canvas.

Enlarging and reducing drawings and photographs

There are different ways of enlarging or reducing photographs and drawings. If you have an ideal photograph it could be photographically enlarged, although you are limited as to what sizes are available from this method. An easier method these days is to make use of one of the commercial enlarging and reducing photocopiers which are readily accessible. These can be used to enlarge or reduce colour prints or black and white photographs to the chosen size, and have made the job of making a correct-sized drawing very much easier.

A very much enlarged picture may look blurred, but so long as you can see the main features of the house, this is really all that matters. In fact, if a lot of the fine detail is lost this is quite a good thing, as it would have to be ignored in the designing of the needlepoint picture anyway, and it is always tempting to try to include much more detail than can possibly be shown in stitchery.

If neither of these methods is available you may be able to use the tried and tested squaring method of enlarging or reducing a picture. To enlarge a picture follow these steps:

1. Divide up your picture into a number of squares.
2. Place the picture in the bottom left hand corner of a blank piece of paper large enough to take the size of picture required.
3. Project a line from the bottom left hand corner of the picture, through the top right hand corner and on to the far edge of the blank sheet.
4. Draw vertical and horizontal lines on the new sheet to meet at this line, to enclose the area required for the new drawing.
5. Divide this new rectangle into the same number of equal squares as the small original.
6. Copy into each square on the large sheet the lines present in the same square on the original small photograph or drawing, increasing their lengths to match the proportions of the bigger square. This will give you your enlarged picture to use as your master drawing.

If you need to reduce a drawing by this method, draw a line from the bottom left corner to the top right corner. Draw vertical and horizontal lines to join each other at this line, enclosing an area of the required size. Draw squares on each picture as for the sizing up process and copy as before.

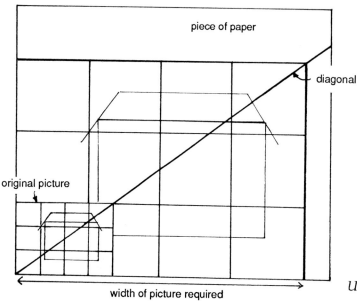

Using the squaring method for enlargement

18

Using an unsuitable picture

If the only picture of the house is one taken from slightly the wrong angle, you will have to draw your own front-on enlarged sketch using the 'unit' method. For this technique you choose one of the features on the house, usually a window, and the width of this feature on the small picture and on the one you are making become your two units of measurement. As the house on the picture you are copying is at an angle, there will be a slight element of guesswork in this method, but if you can look at the real house to check any queries, this need not be too troublesome.

If you are using a window for your unit, decide how wide this window needs to be on the enlarged drawing for the whole picture to be the required size, making sure that this large unit, which will be the width of one or more of the windows on your picture, covers a definite number of threads on the canvas you are using. The picture will then be easy to transfer to the canvas when completed, and easy to sew so that it looks realistic. If you need to show a glazing bar down or across the middle of your window, it is best to have an odd number of threads inside your window frame, so that there is a middle thread along which to sew a line of tent stitches. If an odd number of threads would make the window the wrong size, a glazing bar may be stitched on the surface down the middle of the window after the glass has been represented in stitchery.

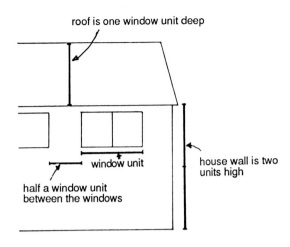

roof is one window unit deep

window unit

half a window unit between the windows

house wall is two units high

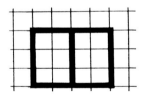

window unit matches thread count (correct)

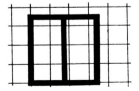

window unit does not match thread count (incorrect)

Choosing the correct window unit size

Using the unit method

Begin your drawing with the roof. Measure on your original picture how many small units (that is, how many widths of the chosen window on the small picture) go to make up first the length and then the depth of the roof. Then with these figures, by using the large unit (that is, the width you have decided on for the same window on the large picture) you can draw the roof of your larger house on the paper.

Having sized up the roof you next need to know how tall the house walls are. You can use multiples of the window unit again, but it may be easier in this case to use the whole roof as your unit. To do this, gauge how many times the height of the roof goes into the height of the house walls. Then draw in your walls to the correct height.

Next put in place the first of your actual windows on the drawing. Use your unit to gauge how far in from the end of the house it needs to be placed and how far down, if at all, from the roof line. Using this unit method for the placing of the other windows, the door, and any other features of the house, your chosen building will gradually emerge on the paper in its correct proportions.

You can, if you wish, miss out the drawing on paper stage, and draw your picture directly on to the canvas. Again, you must first decide how many vertical threads your window unit is going to cover.

Draw on the canvas with an HB pencil, in the same way as you would on paper, measuring carefully the distances between features as you

19

Farmhouse – stitches used:

Sky: Oriental stitch with herringbone satin stitch clouds.

Roof: Jacquard stitch in two shades of grey. The ridge and guttering are in single trammed Gobelin stitch.

Chimneys: Double brick stitch.

House walls: Parisian stitch worked sideways.

Window frames: Tent stitch. The lintels are two rows of tent stitch.

Windows: Diagonal satin stitch.

Door: Single trammed Gobelin stitch.

Climbing rose: Small straight stitches and French knots.

Garden wall: Double brick stitch with plants shown growing on the stonework .

Gate: Tent stitch with graduated sheaf stitch ring in the middle.

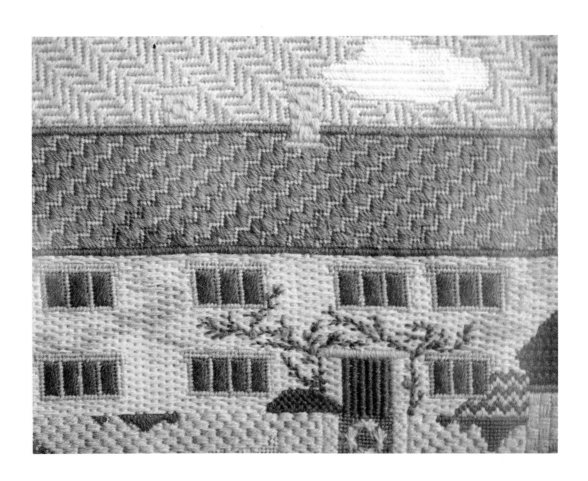

Farmhouse

This picture of her own home was worked by a former student of the author. This house is situated right on a narrow road near a corner, and it was difficult to obtain a good front view picture from which to work, so a working picture had to be drawn using the photo and looking at the actual building. The architecture is typical of the older properties in the south west of Britain, being built of honey-coloured stone with stone-mullioned windows. This picture is worked in crewel wools on 13s interlock canvas.

progress. If you make a mistake it is possible to rub out the lines with a soft rubber.

The garden

With the drawing of the house complete, you may now indicate on the picture which garden features you wish to include. This need only be very sketchy, showing the position of large trees, areas of grass and flower borders. Most of the minor garden features will be worked from the original photograph as the house is being embroidered. If you want to include a tree which comes across the front of the house you must decide whether the tree will completely hide part of the house, or whether the house will be visible through the foliage. If the house is to be visible through the branches, then some, or all of these branches may be worked on top of the finished stitches of the house walls as surface stitchery. If the branches are very large it is probably best to work them on the background and just work the smaller branches and leaves as surface stitchery, as was done in the Lakeland Cottage picture (p.41).

Transferring the picture to the canvas

Now that you have the picture of your house the size you want it on paper, the next step is to transfer this to the chosen canvas.

Go over the lines of the drawing with a dark fibre-tipped pen slightly wider than the canvas mesh, so that the outlines may be clearly seen through the canvas. Choose a piece of canvas several inches (not less than 8 centimetres) wider all round than your picture, so that if you felt it necessary artistically, you could make your picture a slightly different size or shape after you have worked the house. It is difficult to imagine exactly what the house is going to look like once it its worked, so always leave yourself plenty of room for changes of mind about the surroundings. Trees and bushes can be moved and the whole house can be made more or less central in the picture so long as you have left yourself space to manoeuvre. I spend a great deal of time at every stage propping the canvas up several yards away and staring at it to see if any changes are necessary. Also you may wish

to leave yourself room to stitch the title of the picture, and your name and the date. Have a look at the different alphabets later in this book to help you decide how much space you need to leave.

Next prepare your canvas by binding the edges with masking tape purchased from a hardware store. Unfortunately some makes do not stick to the canvas very well, so if possible do a little experimenting.

Place your prepared canvas over the house picture and trace it through on to the canvas with an HB pencil or 'fade-away' pen available from needlework shops. An HB pencil is preferable to anything softer because the graphite of a soft B pencil may come off on to or show through pale coloured threads. If the picture becomes indistinct as you stitch, it can always be placed over the original drawing again and the lines renewed.

Some lines of the main features of the house will fit exactly on to the lines of the canvas mesh, but others will have to be moved slightly to accommodate them to the canvas. Make sure that all windows which in life are the same size are shown as such on the picture.

At this stage you have to think ahead somewhat to the stitches you intend to use, in order to decide whether to draw your lines *on* or *between* the canvas threads. For the house front and roof you will probably be using straight stitches such as brick and Parisian. These stitches end in the holes between the threads, and that is where the outlines for these features should be placed.

On the other hand, it is very likely that you will be outlining the windows in tent stitch, which is made *over* a single canvas thread, so in the case of the window frames, your lines should be made *on* the canvas threads and not between them, as otherwise there may be some confusion as to where to place the stitches when you come to work them. Narrow features such as drainpipes may be shown on the picture, but are best put in after the wall or other background feature has been stitched as then they have the natural three-dimensional look. Their position will be gauged by referring to the original photograph or drawing.

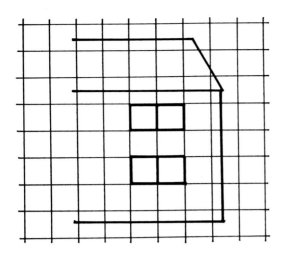

Positioning the drawing on the canvas. Place lines for house walls between the canvas threads if using straight stitches. Place lines for window frames on the canvas threads for tent stitch. (The canvas grid here is not to scale.)

Representation of windows

The windows are the 'eyes' of your house, and how you represent them will make a vital difference to the look of the finished work.

The usual method of outlining the windows is with tent stitch. It is not always possible, because of space restrictions, to make a distinction between the width of the frames and the width of the glazing bars between the panes, which may also be shown in tent stitch. If the window area is too small for a canvas thread to be representative of a glazing bar, then the whole window must be sewn in the glass colour (usually black or dark grey, unless there are obvious curtains showing through the glass) and then the glazing bars may be put on later as surface stitchery, probably using back stitch or one single straight stitch. A thinner thread may be used for these lines, possibly a 'silk' over a woollen base. The stitch used for the window panes may vary, depending on the size of the window. Usually on a window of any size, satin stitch worked diagonally looks the best, but if the windows are very small, as on the American house, then a vertical straight stitch looks neater. If a window is very tiny it may be shown merely by a few vertical threads without any surrounding frame.

Windows which are depicted in dark grey or black are often greatly enhanced by having a small stitch or two in white or pale grey inserted at an angle to look like reflections. Otherwise, a single grey or white thread may be mixed with the dark grey or black threads used for the glass.

Painting the canvas

As mentioned in the section on canvas, it is a good idea to paint your canvas with the appropriate colours if you feel it would help you, though it is not necessary. The only situation when it would be an advantage from the pictorial point of view would be if certain straight stitches did not cover the canvas well and the mesh showed through. In such a case painting would hide the canvas but better coverage could otherwise be achieved by putting an extra thread in the needle.

Georgian Terraced House – stitches used:

Sky: Chevron stitch.

Roof: Single brick stitch in mixed grey and buff. A single long stitch in the same mixture is worked across the front to divide the roof from the walls.

House walls: Brickwork stitch in three mixed shades of honey, gold and buff.

Window frames: Tent stitch, as are the glazing bars.

Windows: Tent stitch worked in a mixture of grey and black.

Railings: Tent stitch. A single straight stitch below the railings is held down at intervals by a small crossing stitch.

Doorway : The arch round the doorway is back stitch in gold. The pillars are horizontal satin stitch in white over two canvas threads, while the brickwork to the outer edges of the pillars is vertical satin stitch in white and gold over two threads. The fanlight is in black tent stitch with white surface stitchery.

Door: Tent stitch and cross stitch.

Steps: Two straight stitches.

Georgian Terraced House

Elegant terraced houses like the one above were an important feature of architecture in Georgian England. They are beautifully proportioned and they usually have interesting doorways with decorative fanlights. On this scale, the intricacies of such features can only be suggested. This picture is worked in 6-strand embroidery floss on 18s interlock canvas.

3 Working the Design

Formal or realistic design?

Having transferred your design on to the canvas, you can now choose whether you are going to try to make your picture look as realistic as possible within the confines of the stitched medium, or whether you would like to work a formal depiction with little pretence at realism.

A formal picture can look very effective in a single colour, in which the stitches alone show up the shapes of the house and its surroundings. For this method the stitches must be carefully chosen, as otherwise the various features will not stand out from each other. For instance, if you choose a vertical stitch for the roof of the house, then it would be wise to choose a horizontal one for the walls. The sky would probably be best in a diagonal stitch, and for the various natural features surrounding the house other contrasting stitches should be chosen, with some motif stitches and French knots for features such as bushes and trees. An Edwardian house worked in a single colour is shown on page 61.

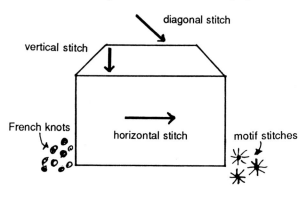

Suggested stitch types on a single-colour picture

Such a picture is very fascinating and it is surprising that even when worked in a woollen thread, the play of light on stitches worked in different directions shows up the shapes of the different features remarkably well. A fairly pale colour should be chosen for a single-colour rendering, as the slight shadows cast would not show on a dark colour. When working in a single pale colour the original picture should be drawn *very* lightly with an HB pencil or preferably in a 'fade-away' pen, as the pencil or any fibre-tipped pen may show through the finished stitchery.

A picture in different tones of the same colour can also be very attractive. The colour may be chosen to fit in with a decorative scheme in your own home or the picture worked in a neutral colour such as sepia tones. Choice of stitches is not so critical with a picture of this type, since although the colours are all tones of the same colour, they do show up against each other if placed carefully. A formal picture may, of course, be just as colourful as a realistic one, but the stitches will be chosen more for their suitability to the overall design than because they look like the subject matter, and there will be no attempt at colour shading and matching to simulate the exact colours of the original. When working a formal picture it is unlikely that you would choose to do any detailed surface stitchery of individual features, as no attempt is being made to make the picture look just like the real house. A formal picture is in essence a design using the various features of the house and garden as the basic elements in the design and could be regarded as an interesting way of presenting a stitch sampler. This being so, if certain features of the actual picture tend to spoil the design, then it would be a good idea to change them, or miss them out altogether. The Alpine chalet (p.65) and the picture of Bruges (p.83) are formal pictures of this type. They do not attempt to show any features which are peculiar to that house, such as different shadings in the fabric of the building, rather they are representative of a certain type of house.

On the other hand in a design attempting realism the stitches are chosen as far as possible to simulate the feature being stitched. Many guidelines are given for this in the next chapter, but you may well come up with completely new ideas of your own which are entirely appropriate. Try all your ideas out, preferably on a spare piece of canvas, as it is often difficult to visualise just what stitches will look like in the colour you have chosen. Try to include as many characteristic details of the house as possible, for this is what will make the picture instantly recognisable, but if there is a feature you absolutely hate, feel free to leave it out. You are the artist after all, and can do whatever you like with your creation. The Country House (p.9) is a good example of a realistic design. In this picture an attempt has been made to show actual patches of lichen on the roof, as well as colour variations in the walls and tiles. The larger the design, the easier it is to show realistic detail, so long as the canvas mesh is fairly small.

Choosing colours

Before you can begin the really exciting part of the project, that is, actually doing the stitching, it is necessary to choose some of the colours you are going to use. Having already transferred your design to canvas, you will have decided whether you are working mainly in mercerised cottons or wools, and whether the picture is to be full colour, single colour or shades of a single colour, but the final colour selection has still to be made.

It is not easy or advisable to try to make the complete selection of colours before you begin stitching, as so often the colours when stitched on the canvas look very different from when they are in hanks. I think you will find that you will change your mind in many cases as to which colour or colour mixture looks best in a certain place, based on the appearance of the picture at the point you have reached.

The first colours to choose are those for the actual house, and these should be matched as closely as possible to the original colour picture, for your house, however correct in shape, is not going to look like the real thing if the colour is completely wrong. To achieve the correct colours it is often necessary to test different colour mixes, and with three strands of wool in the needle there are many different possible mixtures. When mixing colours in the needle, do not use colours very different in tone, or

entirely different in colour, as they will look speckled instead of making a new colour, as would be the case when mixing watercolour paints. Try several mixes out on a spare piece of canvas, and perhaps in the end you will use as many as three or four different mixtures on the walls of the house, as stone, particularly, varies greatly in its colour within a single wall. Similarly the roof, which probably has one or two main colours, may look very patchy owing to weathering and the growth of mosses and lichens. The more you can depict the subtle colours within the various features of the building, the more your needlepoint will look like the real house.

Next choose the basic colours for the garden or other setting of the house. If you are working from a colour photograph you can try to match the colours exactly, but this is not vital and you will be thinking more of what colours will look best on your picture, rather than what the colours looked like in the garden on the day your photograph was taken. Obviously, if the trees are fir trees, it would be foolish to give them the colours of deciduous trees, but you can use artistic licence here, and possibly change the season of the year to suit your preferred colour scheme, or add flowers which actually ceased flowering three months before the photograph was taken.

It is difficult to advise on how much thread you will need of each colour, as when you are mixing the colours in the needle it is well nigh impossible to gauge. However, spare thread is never wasted and it is good to have a bag full of oddments of different colours for shading, flowers and other small features. The colour matching of different dye lots of needlepoint threads seems to be very good, so if you run out of a vital colour it is quite likely that you will be able to match it exactly.

Working areas of patchy colour

If you are working a roof such as that of the Lakeland Cottage (p.41), which has patches of different colour mixes in it, it might seem that you would have to keep stopping and starting with the different mixes in order to keep the pattern correct. So long as you keep to a simple straight stitch such as one of the brick stitches, it

American Single-storey House – stitches used:

Sky: Double twill stitch.

Roof: Single brick stitch with a single straight stitch placed along each edge.

Chimney: Tent stitch.

House walls: Straight satin stitch in white. The hanging baskets are French knots and small straight stitches.

Window frames: Tent stitch.

Windows: Diagonal satin stitch worked in black and grey.

Door: Herringbone satin stitch in burgundy red.

Path: Single trammed Gobelin and mosaic stitch depending on which part of the lawns the path is crossing.

Tree on left: Chinese fan stitches randomly placed, the gaps filled with tent and Gobelin stitch.

Tree on right: Graduated sheaf stitches placed randomly, the gaps filled with tent stitch.

Centre tree: Cross stitch with grey straight stitches for the branches. The sky in this area is worked between the cross stitches after they are in place.

Garden: French knot flowers on bushes and other plants made from straight stitches, chain stitches, cross stitches and upright cross stitches. The background is filled with tent stitch.

Lawns: The centre lawn is mosaic stitch, and the outer lawn is single trammed Gobelin stitch.

American Single-storey House

This is a typical North American house with simple uncluttered lines, surrounded by large areas of grass and highly decorative flower areas. Some of the taller plants have been left out of the foreground of the picture, as they obscured the view of the house. This picture is worked in 6-strand embroidery floss on 18s interlock canvas.

is not difficult to work patches of the same colour-mix in different parts of the roof and then go back and fill in the gaps with other mixes. Work a patch of one desired mix, and then work your way across the canvas to the next area you want to cover with the same mix, by putting in just enough of the brick stitch pattern to enable you to fill in the gaps correctly later with another of your mixtures of colour.

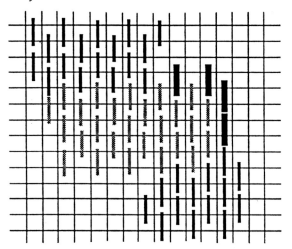

Working areas of patchy colour. The thick lines are the joining stitches between two areas of the same colour-mix.

Order of working

It is always advisable, when working needlepoint pictures, to start with the most important features, in this case, the house. Work the roof first, and then the windows and doors, followed by the house walls, making sure that the stitches, where appropriate, contrast with each other in direction even if you are not working a single-colour picture.

The rest of the picture may be worked in any order, and each particular feature does not need to be fully worked before moving on to the next one. You can work patches here and there if it helps you to get the feel of what the overall picture will look like. Do not concentrate minutely on one aspect of the picture only to realise when you have completed that particular part that it does not look right in the picture as a whole. The shapes of trees and hillsides

should be completed before the sky is stitched up to their edges, because they have definite outlines, whereas the sky just fills in the remainder of the space. Clouds may be worked as separate features, or may be represented by changing the colour mixes in the sky.

Surface stitchery is added after the canvas has been covered with a basic stitch. Its purpose may be to add particular features to the house, such as drainpipes, gutters, door handles, window boxes, hanging baskets or creepers. A drainpipe could be sewn in tent or back stitch at the same time as the walls of the house directly on to the canvas, but actually looks a great deal more authentic if it is embroidered *after* the walls have been finished so that there is a definite three-dimensional element, just as there is in reality. Similarly, it is much better to embroider creepers on to a background of a sewn wall, as then parts of the wall show through in a very realistic way.

Surface stitchery may also be used to great effect in the garden of the picture. Bushes, which may be worked in a simple stitch, can be made to flower abundantly with the addition of a few colourful French knots, and similarly a tree may be given blossom or fruit. A rather flat path can be given texture with tiny knots or a plain stitched lawn may be enlivened by the addition of long grasses and tall flowers, as in the Lakeland Cottage scene (p.41).

There is no end to the details which can be added with surface stitchery, and it is often these little extra touches which have been added when the picture might have been said to have been finished, which make the whole scene come alive and assume an individual character.

4 Which stitch to use

It is often difficult to make the initial decisions as to which stitches are going to look best for the different parts of the house or its surroundings. It is best not to make all these decisions before you begin, because as you go along it will be much easier to see which stitch will look best next to those already in position.

However, there are certainly stitches, which by their shape and direction of stitching, are more suited to some parts of the picture than others, and this chapter aims to help with choices by highlighting the different parts of the picture and suggesting stitches which would look good. Most of these stitches are used in the pictures in this book but some are only shown in the stitch diagrams chapter. No doubt you will in time be able to add to the lists, but they form a good starting point.

Roofs

Many different materials are used for roofing houses, both natural and man-made, as different from each other as corrugated iron, stone tiles and thatch. Each may however be realistically represented by careful choice of stitch.

Single brick stitch is a popular choice as it is small and its regular pattern looks very like small tiles. It may be worked vertically or horizontally, depending on the tile shape.

Lakeland cottage

Brick stitch or double brick stitch may be worked either vertically or horizontally and, with variations in colour, can simulate tiles well. The choice of which brick stitch to use for a roof will depend not only on the size of the actual tile, but also on the scale to which the picture is being worked.

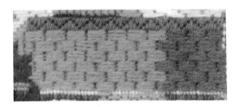

Victorian house

Single trammed Gobelin is an effective stitch for roofs, and may be used either vertically or horizontally, depending on the effect required.

New Zealand waterfront

Waterfall stitch is a useful stitch for simulating thatch, especially if two closely related colours are used together in the needle to give an added textural look.

Thatched cottage

Small Parisian stitch worked sideways makes a neat roof for a house with small tiles as a change from single brick stitch.

Modern bungalow

Other suggested stitches for roofs:
Back (outlining the eaves, as on New Zealand Waterfront houses).
Jacquard (Farmhouse).
Split (outlining, as on North American Weatherboard house).

Satin stitch may be used for a very smooth roof. If some texture is required, the thread may be slightly twisted as you work (Australian Outback house).

House and Garden walls

It is very important in a realistic portrayal of a house to get not only the colours of the walls correct, but also to suggest the texture and if possible the shapes of the materials of which they are constructed.

Several different colours can be mixed in the needle, and unless a very formal picture is required, where areas of solid colour are acceptable, it is always a good idea to mix at least two colours for a feature such as a wall.

Brickwork stitch is the obvious stitch for brick walls of any kind as it is so realistic. The colours can be mixed in the needle to match almost any colour of bricks, which always have colour variations within them.

Victorian red-brick house

Gobelin stitch looks very like weatherboarding, and may be worked over different numbers of threads for different sized boards. Single trammed Gobelin has a similar but more three-dimensional effect.

New Zealand waterfront

Arrowhead stitch may be used sideways to give a smooth effect as in the 1920s semi-detached house picture.

1920s semi-detached house

Parisian stitch worked sideways makes good stone walls. With its regular interlocking format it is easy to simulate the differing colours found in natural stone.

Farmhouse

Water stitch also looks good as walls if a smooth appearance is required. It may be used upright or horizontal.

Lakeland cottage

Other suggested stitches for house and garden walls:

Brick, worked sideways over four or six threads (Edwardian house).
Double brick (Farmhouse, Modern bungalow)
Satin (American single-storey house).

Tent (Australian Outback house).
Single trammed Gobelin for weatherboarding (New England house).
Upright cross (Bruges).

Victorian House – main stitches used:

Sky: Water stitch in blues, greys and white.

Roof: Double brick stitch worked sideways in different shades of grey.

House walls: Rear wall is Parisian stitch worked sideways. Gable wall, constructed of larger, irregular stonework, is worked in Byzantine stitch.

Window frames: Tent stitch, as are the glazing bars.

Windows: Diagonal mosaic stitch in greys, black and white.

Door surround: Oriental stitch.

Door: Cashmere stitch.

Drainpipe: Tent stitch.

Balcony: Cross stitch in white.

Trees on right: Tent stitch, chain stitch, cross stitch, French knots, leaf stitch.

Trees on left: Fan stitch, leaf stitch, chain stitch.

Grass: Brick stitch.

This is a complex picture and it is not possible to itemise every stitch used. It is a good example of the fact that with a little ingenuity, it is possible to get all sorts of effects of perspective and shadows in stitchery.

Victorian House

This handsome Victorian house is the home of a past student of the author, and the picture was worked by her as her first attempt at a needlepoint picture of this type, using as her inspiration a drawing she had made. Both the original photograph and the drawing are shown opposite. A great variety of stitches has been incorporated and the colours are harmoniously blended. This is the only house featured in this book where a perspective view has been used. As the house is an L-shape with a balcony along the projecting part, it would have been difficult to work a realistic view without showing this balcony. It was crucial to the effect that the balcony rails should be worked at the correct angle, and this has been very carefully done. This picture is worked in wools on interwoven canvas.

Windows

The appearance of the windows on a needlepoint picture can make or mar the whole piece of work, so great care must be taken over their representation, and when the finished picture has been stretched they must be their true shape.

It is not always appreciated that glass viewed from outside the house invariably looks dark, although curtains and plants may be seen through the windows showing their own colour, and net curtains can lighten the colour considerably, as in the Victorian red-brick house picture.

Country house

Tent stitch is nearly always used for window frames and glazing bars. Unfortunately the scale of these pictures is not usually large enough for the glazing bars to be made narrower than the frames of the windows.

Satin stitch, either straight or diagonal, is best for the smooth effect needed for glass. A strand of white may be mixed with the dark glass colour to give the effect of reflections.

North American Weatherboard house

Hungarian stitch with diagonal threads stitched between the sections looks very like leaded lights.

Single trammed Gobelin may be worked vertically inside window frames of tent stitch when there is insufficient room to insert glazing bars.

36

Doors

The stitch to be used will depend on what material makes up the door. Sometimes there are glass panels, which should be stitched as described in the previous section on windows.

Wooden panels may be shown by a single square or rectangular stitch or a group of such stitches, depending on the scale of the picture. Bars of straight satin stitch at right angles to each other may also be used.

Tent stitch is best for door frames, and may be used for the entire door, as in the sample opposite.

Victorian red-brick house

Satin stitch in a herringbone pattern is an effective stitch for doors made of vertical boards.

Country house

Cross stitch may be used to simulate panels in doors such as those of the Georgian terraced house.

Georgian terraced house

Single *mosaic stitches* facing alternate ways may be used to represent glass panels in doors.

Other suggested stitches for doors:
Twill or double twill. Do not use twill stitch over two horizontal canvas threads, as it looks exactly the same as single brick.
Single brick stitch is good for a very plain door.

Alpine chalet

Fences, hedges and railings

Wooden fences may be of several types, but are usually constructed in sections with uprights in between. Hedges may be neat and flat in appearance or bushy and untidy. Different stitches can be chosen to suit all these different forms. If a hedge or fence is being shown with a garden behind it, it is best to work the hedge first and then stitch the background up to it.

Single trammed Gobelin stitch may be worked vertically to form the uprights for panelled fencing. Also shown here is diagonal satin stitch worked in a herringbone pattern to make good fencing panels.

Edwardian house

Hungarian stitch makes an interesting hedge with an undulating top. Mix two colours in the needle for the best effect.

1920s semi-detached house

Fly stitch worked vertically and close together makes a realistic hedge of closely growing trees, especially if two or more colours of green are mixed in the needle.

Thatched cottage

Upright cross stitch may be worked into many different shapes ideal for formal hedging.

Other suggested stitches for fences, hedges and railings:

Tent stitch is useful for uprights of all sorts of fencing.

Double brick stitch worked sideways would look good as interwoven fencing.

Tent stitch is best for railings, perhaps with added French knots (Victorian red-brick).

38

Trees

Many different ways of depicting trees are needed, so that variety can be introduced into the landscape surrounding the house. Stitches to be used vary according to whether the trees are in the foreground where detail is required, or in the background where only outlines, or the impression of a mass of trees are to be shown.

Leaf stitch may be used for trees of many different shapes, both fir and deciduous, and is suitable for formal and informal pictures.

North American weatherboard house

Country house

Fan stitches, because of their ragged edge, can be formed into very realistic-looking deciduous trees, while random types of fan stitch of different sizes make good surface-stitched leaves. Different effects are achieved with the same stitch in the two examples shown here.

Lakeland cottage

French knots, if closely packed, can form whole trees, looking best as small formal trees with contrasting French knot fruits or flowers.

Thatched cottage

Lakeland Cottage – stitches used:

Sky: Chevron stitch in mixed blues, whites and pale greys.

Hillside: Diagonal ground stitch in various grass-green colour mixtures.

Roof: Single brick stitch worked sideways, using various mixtures of dark greys, greens and deep gold to suggest the moss and lichens on the slates.

Chimneys: Vertical brick stitch. Different colours were used for the two chimneys to show the varying building materials used. The sides of the chimneys are in diagonal satin stitch.

Walls: Water stitch worked vertically in pure white to give a flat look to the walls as on the photograph.

Window frames: Worked in tent stitch, as are the glazing bars. An edging has been worked on the right hand sides to show that the windows are recessed.

Windows: Diagonal satin stitch worked in iron grey. Curtains are shown at the windows by straight stitches at various angles.

Door: Black herringbone satin stitch.

Porch: Split stitch uprights with satin stitch top.

Climbing rose: Straight stitches and French knots.

Garden wall: Water stitch in various colour mixes of grey and dark brown, deep gold and green. The top of the wall is diagonal satin stitch.

Tree on left: The trunk and branches are closely packed stem stitches in various dark colour mixes. The leaves are random fan-type stitches added as surface stitchery on top of the sky and hillside.

Tree on right: Upright graduated sheaf stitches on a background of tent and Gobelin stitches.

Foreground: The grass is woven plait stitch in two colours of green with surface random straight stitches and French knots. The garden path is massed French knots and the bush on the right is random groups of straight stitches.

Lakeland Cottage

This is a typical English Lakeland cottage with whitewashed walls and a slate roof. Such cottages now boast all modern conveniences, but at the time the photograph was taken, the only running water was a pump in the kitchen, the 'facilities' were housed in a shed at the end of the garden, and cooking and lighting were by paraffin. The original picture here was an old black and white photograph, so the colours were chosen from memory and from a more recent colour print of the cottage. This picture is worked in crewel wools on 13s interlock canvas.

New Zealand waterfront

Florentine stitch, randomly worked in mounds of different colours of green, may be used for large areas of trees in the background of a picture.

Chinese fan stitches can be set into a background of small random diagonal stitches.

American single-storey house

Other suggested stitches for trees:
Single cross stitch for dense patches of greenery, as on fir trees.
Fly stitch and *random fly stitch* (North American weatherboard house).
Leaf stitch variations (Alpine chalet).
Graduated sheaf stitches under each other, in rings (Edwardian house), or set into a tent stitch background (American single-storey house).

Byzantine and *mosaic stitches* may also be used for trees (Thatched cottage, Modern bungalow).
Stem and *random straight stitches* are useful for tree trunks (Lakeland cottage).
Single trammed Gobelin may be used for narrow, straight tree trunks (Thatched cottage).

Bushes, creepers and flowers

The small features which are added to the garden and house when the main features are in place are very important, as they often give the whole picture a 'lift', and can change a rather ordinary picture into something quite stunning.

Bushes, creepers and flowers give little areas of colour and interest and can be added until you are happy that the effect is as good as could possibly be achieved. Most of these small items are best added when the main features are in place, as it always looks good to have a little of the background showing through.

The *French knot* is the most useful stitch for the smaller plants in the picture. Knots in a variety of appropriate colours may be used to liven up any rather dull corner of the house or garden with a riot of flowers or creepers.

American single-storey house

The *bullion knot* is a handsome three-dimensional stitch and can be used to make a bush of any shape.
These knots look best worked into rounded shapes radiating out from a central point.

Bruges

French knots on stalks make unusually shaped bushes. They look their best when formed radiating out from a point or short baseline. They may be worked in mixed colours, and extra French knots can be interspersed if required.

Bruges

Chain stitches placed singly can also be made into a bush of any shape, perhaps with small French knot flowers.

Country house

Random straight stitches may be used for bushes as a contrast to some of the more compact and rounded stitches.

Lakeland cottage

Other suggested stitches for bushes, creepers and flowers:

Detached *fly stitches* (Country house).
Back stitch (Country house).
Stem stitch (Lakeland cottage).
Cross stitch.
Single cross stitch.

North American Weatherboard House – stitches used:

Sky: Diagonal mosaic stitch in mixed blues with white added for the cloud effect.

Roof: Outlined in split stitch.

Chimney: Single brick stitch outlined in back stitch.

Walls: Single trammed Gobelin in champagne colour.

Window frames: Worked in tent stitch, as are the glazing bars on the larger windows. The bars on the small windows are single straight stitches.

Windows: Diagonal satin stitch worked in iron grey. A few flashes of white have been stitched into the grey to look like reflections. A plant in cross stitch with a French knot flower is shown at one of the downstairs windows.

Door: White herringbone satin stitch inside a tent stitch frame. The glazed window is in iron grey diagonal satin stitch.

Steps: Tent stitch and Gobelin stitch.

Climbing rose: Straight stitches and French knots.

Trees on left: Mainly made up from leaf stitches worked together into different shapes. The tree trunks are worked in parallel straight stitches of mixed grey and brown. Fir cones are French knots.

Tree on right: The tree on the right is worked in a random type of fly stitch to give the typical fir tree outline.

Foreground: Arrowhead stitch in two colours of grass green.

Flowers: Straight stitch and French knot flowers grow over a low random straight stitch wall.

North American Weatherboard House

This weatherboard house is situated in a clearing in the forests of western Canada, and is built largely of local materials. As the setting is so wooded, there is no garden as such, but a good splash of colour is provided by the flowers planted up against the house walls. The stairway to the left allows access to the upper storey. This picture is worked in crewel wools on 13s interlock canvas.

Lawns, paving, gravel, fields, hillsides, bare earth and mountains

These are foreground or background features and therefore in some cases need to be bold and in other cases less significant. Foreground features can be worked in larger stitches and brighter colours, whereas those in the background should be smaller patterns and more misty colours.

It is often stated that backgrounds should be darker than foregrounds, but when you actually look at landscapes, it seems that the colours in the distance are not necessarily dark, but rather lose their clarity. In temperate countries they become misty greys tinged with blues or violets, while in hot climates distant views can seem misty ochres and terracottas. Foreground colours, on the other hand, are always more vibrant.

Australian Outback house

Hungarian diamonds are ideal for a bold foreground of grass or bare earth. See also the Alpine chalet picture.

North American weatherboard house

Arrowhead is a large straight stitch which looks good as a foreground. Mix different colours of green in the needle for the varied colours of grass.

Lakeland cottage

Woven plait stitch makes an unusual design and can form an interesting foreground, possibly as a base for other stitches.

Jacquard stitch, with its diagonal appearance, is a good stitch to use for a sloping field or hillside.

Alpine chalet

Mountain stitch, as its name implies, was developed for depicting alpine scenery. Use several different shades of the colour you choose, and make sure you cover the whole canvas with the blocks of colour.

Alpine chalet

Other suggested stitches for lawns, paving, gravel, fields, hillsides, bare earth and mountains:

Diagonal ground is useful for sloping fields and hillsides (Lakeland cottage).

Hungarian is a neat stitch for foregrounds of paving, gravel or bare earth and for far hillsides (Australian Outback house).

Mosaic is very neat and especially suitable for small pictures (American single-storey house).

Single trammed Gobelin stitch has a three dimensional appearance which can form a useful contrast to flatter stitches (American single-storey house, Australian Outback house).

Small Parisian stitch is a neat stitch for a formal lawn (Thatched cottage).

Oblique Slav stitch is suitable for a smooth distant hillside (Australian Outback house).

Massed tiny *French knots* make good gravel effects (Lakeland cottage).

Water

Many different colours are always present in views of water, and these variations shquld be shown in the picture to give any look of realism. Both the stitches given here make it possible to include a variety of shades. If a very formal scene is being depicted, other stitches could be used without colour mixing.

Water stitch is a horizontal straight stitch worked in such a way that the thread is not split, which would spoil the effect.

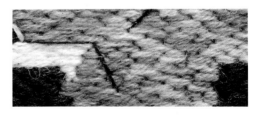

New Zealand waterfront

Waterfall stitch is a straight stitch which may be used vertically or horizontally. It is possible to mix different colours and strands of thread to achieve a very smooth effect.

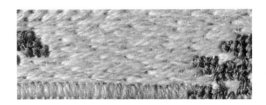

Australian Outback house

Thatched Cottage – stitches used:

Sky: Twill stitch in blue with a few strands of white inserted to form a cloud.

Roof: Waterfall stitch in a mixture of gold and buff coloured threads. A line of back stitches just below the top of the roof shows where the thatch is held down, and a small bird on the roof is the thatcher's mark.

Chimney: Brickwork stitch in a terracotta colour to simulate brick. The chimney pot is satin stitch with a strand of black outlining it against the sky.

House walls: The straight black timbers are tent stitch, while the diagonal ones are single straight stitches. The infilling is in white diagonal satin stitch.

Window frames: Tent stitch, as are the glazing bars.

Windows: Tent stitch in grey with small strands of black for reflections.

Door: Herringbone satin stitch.

Hedge: The hedge next to the house is vertical rows of upright fly stitches in two shades of green mixed in the needle. The small hedge at the front of the garden is in upright cross stitch, while the side hedging is long legged cross stitch.

Path: Small French knots in shades of grey.

Gate: Tent and straight stitches.

Lawn: Small Parisian stitch worked sideways.

Trees and flowers: The tree trunk is single trammed Gobelin, while the top is French knots, and the background behind it is single brick stitch. The mass of blossom to the right of the house is mosaic stitch in a mixture of pink and green. The flowers are French knots.

Thatched Cottage

Thatched cottages are always picturesque, and even if you do not live in one, they make ideal subjects for pictures. Being half timbered as well as thatched, this particular cottage combines two very ancient building methods, and good examples of this type of dwelling are becoming increasingly difficult to find. This picture is worked in 6-strand embroidery floss on 18s interlock canvas.

Skies

The importance of the sky in a picture varies enormously. In a small miniature in embroidery silks, the sky often need only be the right colour to tone in with the main picture, and be worked in an interesting and appropriately sized stitch. In a larger picture, the sky can be an important feature and, if working with wools, there are great opportunities for shading and including realistic cloud effects, either as separate entities in different stitches, or incorporated into the stitch used for the sky. Usually a diagonal stitch, or a stitch which looks diagonal, is most appropriate.

Chevron stitch is a useful stitch in that it looks like a diagonal stitch, but as it is actually straight, it does not distort the canvas. It is possible to achieve good cloud effects when using this stitch.

Modern bungalow

Milanese stitch is a favourite for skies as its wavy effect can only be seen when quite a large area is being worked.

Country house

Diagonal ground stitch may be used for the sky, but does tend to distort the canvas easily if used over a large area. This distortion can of course be straightened out at the finishing stage, but it is best to leave the sky until the last if this stitch has been chosen.

Edwardian house

Double twill stitch is a very good one to use for skies, as is twill stitch itself. Both are straight stitches which do not distort the canvas, yet they step down the canvas diagonally. Different shades can easily be worked into skies using this stitch.

Alpine chalet

Other suggested stitches for skies:
Twill (Thatched cottage).
Florentine (Australian Outback house).
Oriental (Farmhouse).

Brick stitches (Sepia tones cottage).
Cashmere stitch (Victorian red-brick house).
Diagonal mosaic stitch (Decorative brick house).

5 *Stitch diagrams*

All the stitches used in the needlepoint pictures or mentioned in the text in this book are described here in detail. By following the numbering and working instructions carefully you will find it easy to use any of these stitches in your own pictures. The colour picture shows a small sample of each stitch. Larger areas of some stitches are shown in the chapter on Which Stitch to Use.

Arrowhead

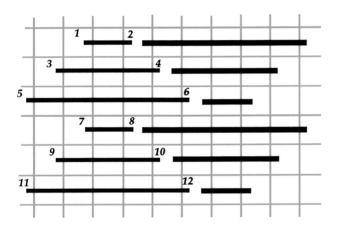

Arrowhead is an easy stitch to work and does not distort the canvas. Work horizontal arrowheads over 2, 4 and 6 canvas threads, the longest stitch of the second row abutting the shortest stitch of the first row. Arrowhead may be used sideways if required.

Back

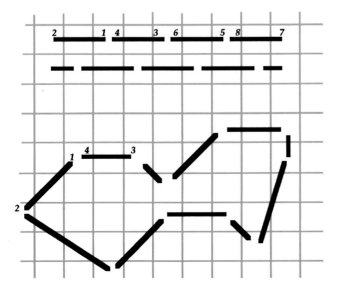

As the name implies, each back stitch is worked back towards the previous stitch, the thread being taken behind and beyond the previous stitch to emerge further along the direction of sewing, ready for the next back stitch. It is useful for outlining and giving neat edges to various features.

Brick

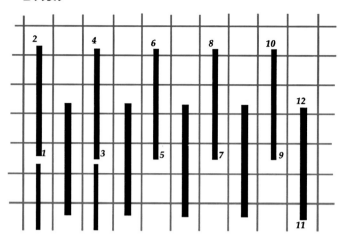

Work in an 'over and over' fashion following the numbers on the diagram. If you want to work patches of a particular colour-mix at some distance from each other, as in a roof like Lakeland Cottage, see instructions in the chapter Working the Design. Brick stitch is quick and easy to work, but may need an extra thread in the needle to cover the canvas well. This stitch may also be worked over six threads of canvas.

Brick, single

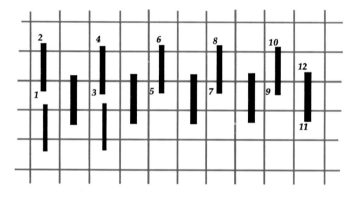

Work in an 'over and over' fashion over two horizontal canvas threads, following the numbering on the diagram, otherwise follow the instructions for brick stitch above.

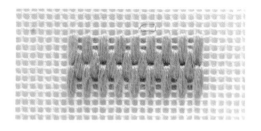

Brick, double

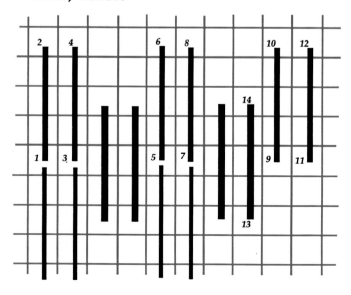

Double brick stitch is worked in exactly the same way as brick stitch, except that two bars are laid down each time instead of one. Be sure to leave three vertical canvas threads between each pair of stitches to allow for the stitches of the row below.

Brickwork

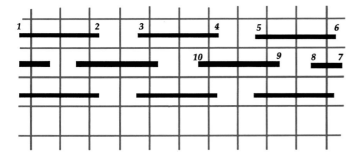

This is a simple interweaving stitch over three threads of canvas and under one. The second row alternates to give the realistic brickwork effect. If very small bricks are required the stitch may be worked over and under one thread only and the rows alternated as in the larger stitch.

Bullion

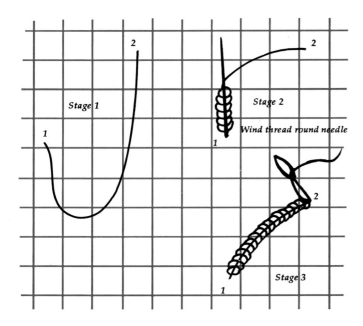

This gives a dramatic three-dimensional effect and may be made any length required. The needle is brought to the front at 1 and taken down again at 2, the distance between 1 and 2 being the length of the stitch. Leave the thread very loose between 1 and 2. The point of the needle is then brought out again at 1 and the loose wool is wound round the needle enough times to fill the space between 1 and 2. Holding the loops of wool, pull the needle through to the front and then to the back again at 2. Arrange the loops tidily on the thread.

Byzantine

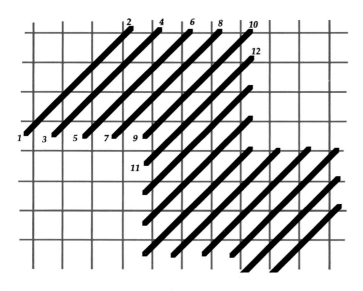

This stitch is made up of steps of diagonal satin stitches. The steps may be of equal or unequal length but are usually of the same depth, a stitch over four intersections of the canvas being common. The rows may the same or contrasting colours. This stitch will distort the canvas if used over a large area. Keep the stitches evenly taut for a smooth effect.

53

Cashmere

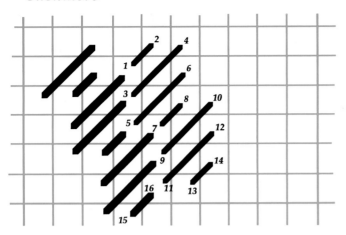

Cashmere is a neat stitch which runs down the canvas in a steep diagonal line. It is worked in groups of four stitches over 1, 2, 2 and 1 intersections of the canvas as on the diagram. The placing of the stitches at the beginning of succeeding rows can be quite tricky, so place first a short stitch which comes one thread down and two threads to the left of the last short stitch of the previous row.

Chain

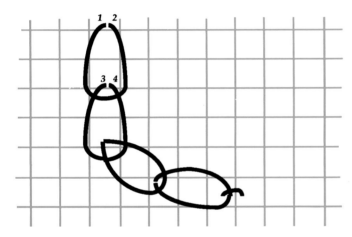

Chain stitch can form a line of stitches in any direction, or separate links may be used at random. Bring the needle and thread to the front of the work. While holding a loop of thread take the needle to the back again through the same hole, and then out to the front where the end of the stitch is required, taking the needle through the loop of thread. If only one link is required, push the needle through to the back of the canvas over the loop and one canvas thread, otherwise work as before.

Chevron

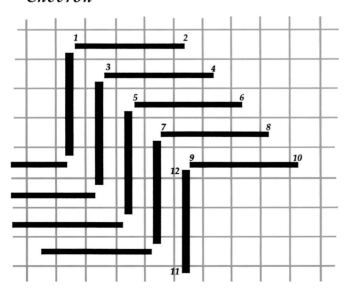

Chevron is a straight stitch in which alternate rows are worked at right angles to each other. As the stitches, usually over four canvas threads, step diagonally down the canvas chevron has the appearance of a diagonal stitch, without the disadvantages of distorting the canvas. An extra strand of thread may need to be used in the needle if really close coverage is required.

Chinese Fan

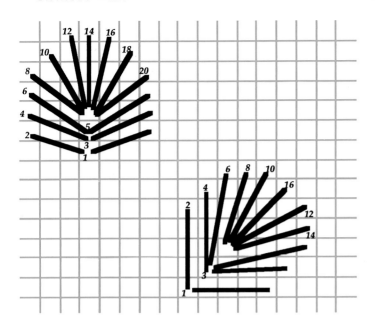

This is a type of leaf stitch with a rounded top and may be worked vertically, diagonally or horizontally. Follow the numbering on the diagram, keeping the thread taut so that it does not mask the hole you need to use. In the diagonal version the top middle stitch should be put in last of the five stitches made from the same hole.

Cross

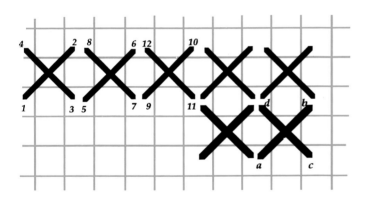

This traditional stitch consists of a cross made over two intersections of the canvas in each direction. Make sure that the same arm is uppermost in each cross unless you choose to have it otherwise.

Cross, long legged

Long legged cross has a rope-like appearance and is made by a short diagonal stitch over two vertical canvas threads being worked on top of a long diagonal stitch over four vertical and two horizontal canvas threads. A small version may be used over one horizontal canvas thread. In this case the short stitch is over one vertical thread and the long stitch over three.

Long Legged Cross Variation

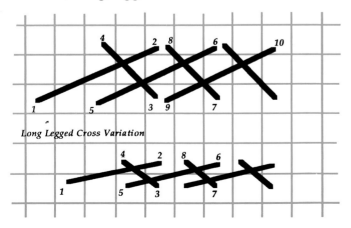

55

Australian Outback House – stitches used:

Sky: A simple Florentine pattern in shades of blue-grey.

Roof: Sloping satin stitches in which the wool is slightly twisted to give the effect of ridges.

Chimney: Tent stitch.

Gable: Outlined with split stitches. The end of the gable is satin stitch.

House walls: Tent stitch.

Window frames: Straight stitches with only two of strands of wool in the needle.

Windows: Tent stitch. Note that the glazing bars of the window on the left are the threads of the canvas itself. On the right-hand window they are single-strand surface stitches.

Door: Tent stitch in two shades.

Fence: Back stitch.

Foreground: Hungarian diamonds in various shades of golden brown and tan.

Area round the house: Single trammed Gobelin in gold and yellow colours.

Trees: These are gum trees worked in single cross stitch with straight stitch trunks and branches.

Creek: Waterfall stitch worked sideways in a mixture of blues and turquoise.

Hillsides: The left-hand hillside is oblique Slav stitch and the right-hand one is Hungarian stitch.

Australian Outback House

Depicting a farm at Burra Creek, South Australia, this picture forms a contrast with all the others in the book, except the Alpine chalet, in that the background to the house is as important to the scene as the house itself. The house is thus shown in its majestic setting, with the creek behind. The hot colours form a contrast to the other settings of houses illustrated in this book. This picture is worked in crewel wools on 13s interlock canvas.

Cross, single

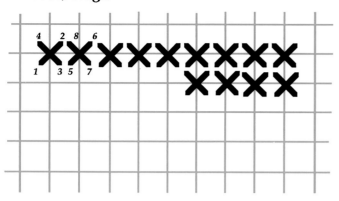

Single cross is a very small firm stitch made in two parts over one intersection of the canvas, as shown on the diagram. To keep the stitch looking even, ensure that the same diagonal is on top in each cross. If a large area is to be covered, it might be necessary to reduce the number of threads in the needle to prevent overcrowding.

Cross, upright

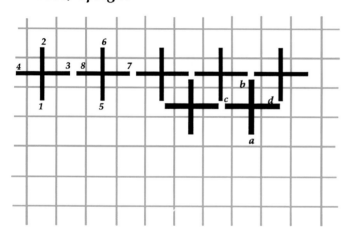

Upright cross makes a firm interlocking stitch in which the upright and horizontal parts of the stitch are both made over two canvas threads. The tops of the vertical stitches of the second and succeeding rows are made into the holes where the horizontal stitches of the preceding row meet. Some interesting shapes can be built up by use of this stitch.

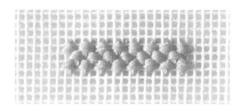

Diagonal ground

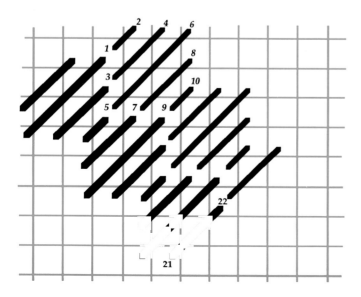

This simple diagonal stitch is worked across 1,2,3 and 2 intersections of the canvas, the sequence then being repeated. Distortion of the canvas will occur if large areas of diagonal ground are worked together, but its usefulness outweighs this slight disadvantage.

Fan

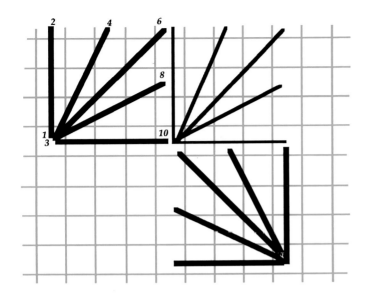

Fan stitch is made up of five arms radiating out from the bottom corner of a square of four threads in each direction. The fan may be stitched facing either way. Smaller fans can be made over three canvas threads, though if larger ones are made the coverage is poor.

Fly

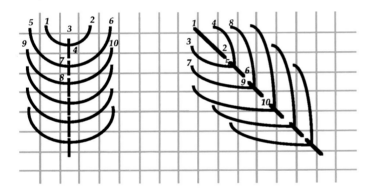

Each loop of fly stitch is held down by a retaining stitch, as illustrated. Follow the numbering carefully, noting that the top of each retaining stitch is in the same hole as the bottom of the one above it. Fly stitch may be made any length and can be vertical, horizontal or diagonal in direction.

Florentine

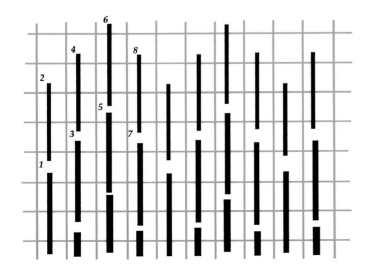

Florentine stitches are made up of a series of straight parallel stitches of the same or varying lengths which usually form a repeating pattern, but which may be used randomly if desired. To achieve a smooth surface, the stitches must be worked evenly in an 'over and over' fashion.

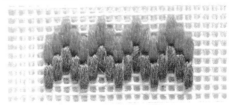

Edwardian House – stitches used:

Sky: Diagonal ground stitch.

Roof: Single brick stitch outlined with long straight stitches held down at intervals.

Chimney: Horizontal satin stitch.

House walls: Brick stitch over six threads worked sideways. Two long horizontal stitches held down at intervals indicate the course of stonework under the windows.

Window frames: Tent stitch, as are the glazing bars. The centre window has been slightly reduced in size, since had it been larger by one more canvas mesh, it would have been too close to the top of the door, and would also have been difficult to divide into equally sized panes.

Windows: Diagonal satin stitch.

Door: Twill stitch outlined in tent stitch, with a line of single trammed Gobelin over the top to indicate the porch.

Path: Hungarian stitch.

Fence: Herringbone satin stitch makes up the fencing panels, while the posts are single trammed Gobelin with French knots on the top.

Tree on the left: Interlocking leaf stitches, with mosaic stitch filling the area between it and the fence.

Tree on the right: Graduated sheaf stitch rings with tent stitch filling. Diagonal mosaic stitch fills the area between tree and fence.

Foreground: Hungarian stitch.

Edwardian House

This is a good type of house to choose to work in a single colour as the features are comparatively simple and are easily shown by differing stitches in one colour. If the design is any more complex than this it is impossible to distinguish the different features and the picture then looks like a sampler of stitches with no particular form. It is important when working with a single colour to follow certain principles, making sure that the major features such as sky, roof and walls are worked in stitches which contrast well with each other in direction, and thus make the features stand out from each other. These principles are explained in Chapter 3. This picture is worked in crewel wools on a 13s interlock canvas.

French knot

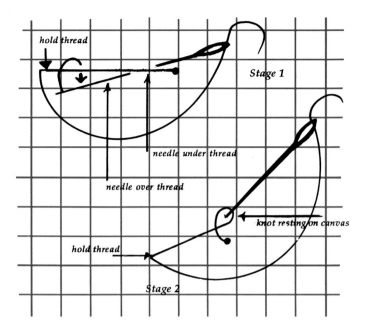

French knots are very useful, and not difficult to work if the technique is practised carefully. Anchor the thread at the back, then with the needle and thread at the front of the work, hold the thread out firmly and pass the needle round it one or more times. Then run the resulting knot down the needle to rest on the canvas as the needle is pulled through an adjacent hole to the back of the work.

French knot on stalk

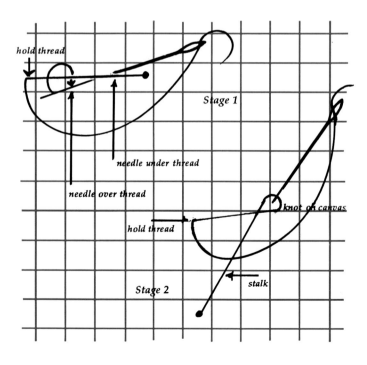

French knots on stalks are made in the same way as French knots except that before the needle is pushed through to the back of the canvas, the stalk is pulled out to the required length and held firmly as the knot is finished off. The knot may be made with one, two or three turns round the needle.

Gobelin

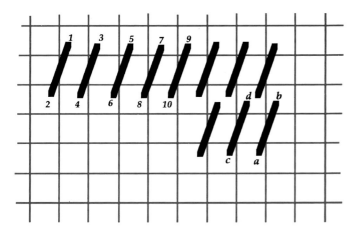

Gobelin stitches are parallel diagonal stitches worked over either two or four horizontal threads and one vertical thread of canvas. The stitches are made in the same way as tent stitches, so that there is a firm covering on the back of the canvas. Work with an even tension to achieve a smooth surface.

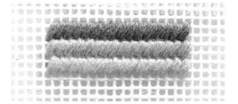

Gobelin, single trammed

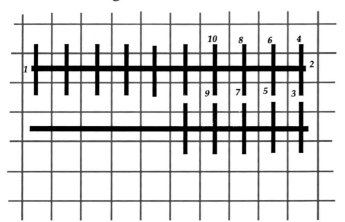

The three-dimensional appearance of this stitch is owing to the tramming thread behind the vertical stitches. Having laid down the tramming thread with a firm tension but no buckling of the canvas, the stitches are worked across it vertically over two canvas threads. Always work the rows in the same direction for a uniform effect. The stitch may be worked horizontally or vertically.

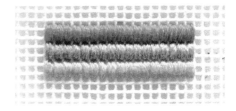

Graduated sheaf

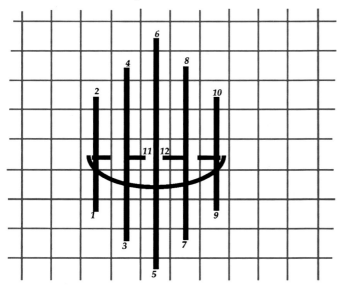

Graduated sheaf may be worked on its own, in lines one above the other, or four may be worked at right angles to each other to form a ring. Five threads are laid down across 4,6,8,6,4 canvas threads. The thread is then brought to the front of the work through the middle hole under the centre thread, the threads being held aside to show this. The needle is slipped under the threads to one side, over the top of the stitch, under the threads at the other side and to the back again through the same hole. Pull tightly to 'bind the sheaf'.

Alpine Chalet – stitches used:

Sky: Double twill stitch in a mixture of two shades of blue.
Mountains: Mountain stitch in white and two shades of pale turquoise.
Roof outline: Back stitches.
Gable end: Diagonal satin stitch worked in two different directions from the centre.
Chimney: Single brick stitch in mixed brown and buff colours.
House front between upper windows: Herringbone satin stitch.
House front between upper and lower windows: Upright single trammed Gobelin.
Lower house front : Waterfall stitch in white.
Shutters: Diagonal satin stitch.
Windows: Individual mosaic stitches in dark grey, with tent stitch glazing bars where there is room.
Side of steps and stone pillar supporting roof: Single brick stitch worked sideways.
Doors: Outlined in tent stitch with small herringbone satin stitch panels. Windows as described above.
Flowers and hanging basket: French knots and single chain stitches.
Logs: Double French knots.
Inside log store: Twill stitch in black.
Hillsides: Jacquard stitch.
Foreground: Hungarian diamonds with French knots in white and yellow.
Trees: Leaf stitch and variations.
Path: Upright cross stitch in grey-green.

Alpine Chalet

Chalets, with their distinctive roofs designed to cope with heavy snowfalls, make interesting subjects for needlepoint. Here, as with the Australian Outback picture, the setting is as important as the house, and the magnificent alpine scenery is the perfect backdrop. Even if you do not live in a chalet, this subject could perhaps make a good memento of a holiday. The source picture shows no mountains, so these have been added, as an alpine chalet without the Alps would not seem quite authentic! The front of the chalet has been simplified, various ornaments and tubs of flowers having been removed and the windows reduced in number. Alterations such as this may be made when a picture is intended to show a certain type of house rather than one particular house. This picture is worked in crewel wools on 13s interlock canvas.

Hungarian

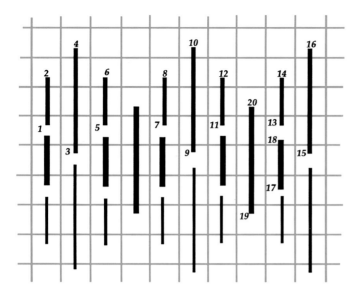

Hungarian stitch forms a small and neat pattern and is very easy to work. The basic motif is stitched over 2,4,2 horizontal canvas threads. A gap of one hole (two threads) is then left for the longest stitch of the next row before the motif is repeated. When working the following rows, notice that all the long stitches come under each other, as do all the short, and no stitch is worked under the long stitches of the preceding row.

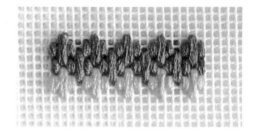

Hungarian diamonds

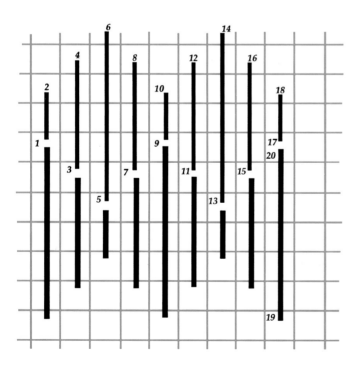

Hungarian diamonds is a much larger stitch than Hungarian, as the longest stitch is over six threads instead of four. It is very easy to work as no gaps have to be left. Stitches are made over 2,4,6,4 horizontal canvas threads, and the sequence is then repeated. On the following rows the longest stitch is under the shortest of the preceding row, and the shorter stitch is under the longest.

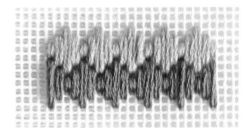

Jacquard

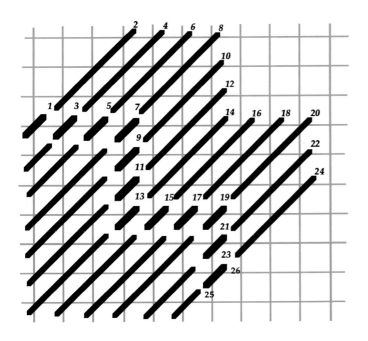

Jacquard is a stepped stitch with parallel satin stitches being made over two or three canvas intersections in the first row, and over one intersection in the second and following alternate rows. The steps may be made any width, the degree of steepness of the stitch down the canvas depending on the width of the steps.

Leaf

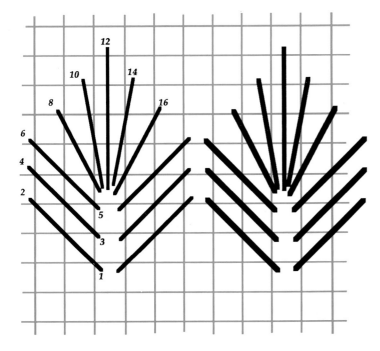

Leaf stitches may be made singly, or arranged together to form large motifs. The sequence of numbering must be followed carefully to achieve the correct three-dimensional form. Note that the first three and the final three stitches are parallel satin stitches across three intersections of the canvas. Also that the five stitches round the top of the leaf all start from the same hole and step down or up one intersection of the canvas from each other.

67

Leaf variations

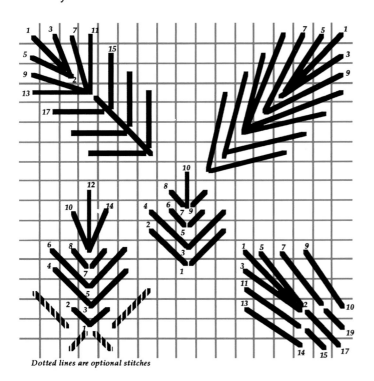

Dotted lines are optional stitches

Five different variations on the leaf shape are illustrated and numbered for ease of working. The diagonal leaves may be worked facing either way, and in some cases four leaves may be joined at their bases to form a motif.

Milanese

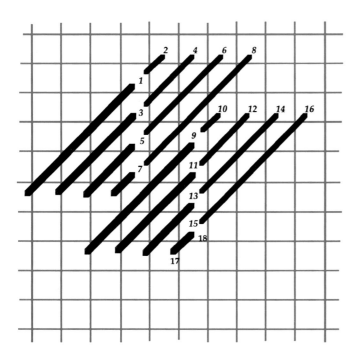

This is a large, handsome diagonal stitch made by working stitches across 1,2,3,4 intersections of the canvas and then repeating the sequence. The shortest stitch of the second and succeeding rows lies up against the longest stitch of the preceding row, thus making the arrowheads face the opposite direction. This stitch needs to be worked over quite a large area for the full wavy effect to be apparent.

Mosaic

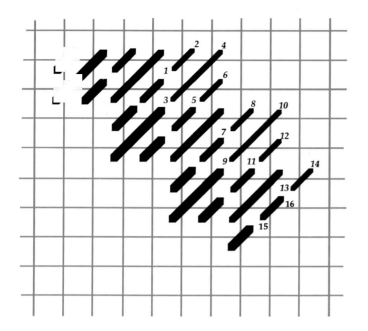

Mosaic stitch when worked has the appearance of neat lines of cross stitches without the three-dimensional element. It is worked diagonally in groups of three stitches over 1,2,1 intersections of the canvas. A gap is left for the longest stitch of the next row before the sequence is repeated.

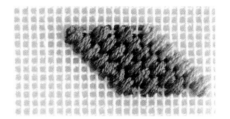

Mosaic, diagonal

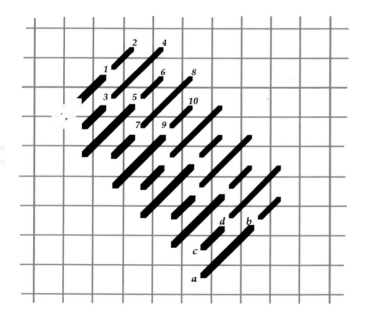

This useful diagonal stitch is worked over 1,2 canvas intersections and then repeated. The long stitches of the second and succeeding rows are worked up against the short stitches of the preceding row. Diagonal mosaic has a more ridged appearance than mosaic stitch and will distort the canvas if used over large areas.

Victorian Red-brick House – stitches used:

Sky: Cashmere stitch.

Roof: Single brick stitch worked sideways with some ochre-coloured threads here and there to create the impression of lichens growing on the slates.

Chimney: Brickwork stitch in a slightly redder mixture of colours than the house walls.

Gable: Outlined in back stitch, black and white, with the inside shape also represented in back stitches. The tiling in the gable end is upright cross stitch in a deep red and grey mixture.

House walls: Brickwork stitch in two colours of terracotta and a single strand of grey.

Window frames: Tent stitch, as are the glazing bars.

Windows: Straight satin stitch worked in various mixtures of black, grey, and white, depending on whether the effect of net curtains is required.

Door: The whole doorway is in tent stitch, mainly black, with the shape of the door outlined in dark green. The dark colours indicate that the doorway is set back from the level of the main front of the house. The door and window lintels are vertical satin stitch.

Drainpipe: The black drainpipe is in back stitch, but the pink one is a single strand of cotton taken down the surface of the house wall.

Garage door: Herringbone satin stitch.

Gate and railings: Mainly in tent stitch. The gate and top rail of the railings are stitched on to the bare canvas, but the upright railings and the French knots representing the ornate ironwork are added as surface stitchery. The wall is brickwork stitch in grey and terracotta.

Pavement in foreground: Hungarian stitch.

Tree and bushes: The tree is single cross stitch and the bushes are French knots.

Victorian Red-brick House

This is a very familiar type of house built in the Victorian era and has many attractive features which can be shown on a needlepoint picture. The details which make the house so interesting are the gable, the bay windows and the intricate railings on the wall in front of the small garden. The shape of the bay windows is quite difficult to show in this two-dimensional format, but the problem has been overcome by use of a slight change in the colour of the bricks where the flat area between the large upper and lower windows of the bay meets the angled panels of bricks between the side windows of the bay. Extra grey strands of cotton in the mixture of threads create the illusion of an angle in the brickwork. The bay window in the 1920s semi-detached house has been worked slightly differently, an actual break being made in the stitchery. This Victorian house picture is worked in 6-strand embroidery floss on 18s interlock canvas.

Mountain

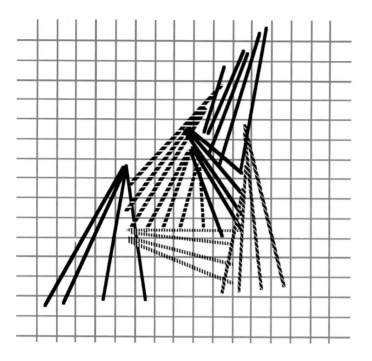

Mountain stitch was developed to give the effect of an uneven mountain side with its varying planes. Groups of straight stitches in more or less triangular shapes are placed at angles to each other, the ends of the stitches usually being placed under those already in position. The stitches should be worked in an 'over and over' fashion, and should not split threads already on the canvas.

Oblique Slav

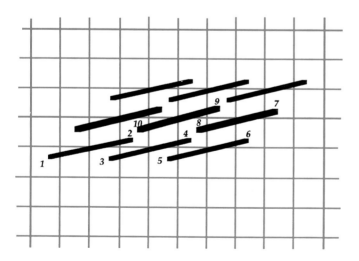

Oblique Slav stitch has a very smooth surface and the individual stitches, which slope only a little from the horizontal, are fitted neatly up against those of the row below. This stitch is most easily worked from bottom to top of the canvas. The work may be turned upside down to work alternate rows if this is found to be easier. The stitches cover three vertical threads and one horizontal. Follow the numbering on the diagram and keep an even tension.

Oriental

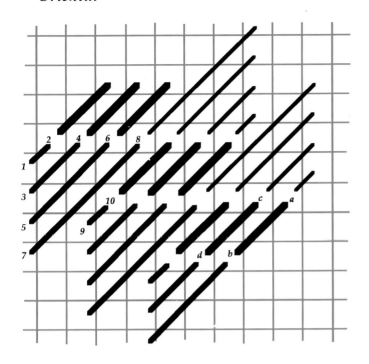

Oriental is a large, flowing stitch which needs to be worked over a large area for maximum effect. The first part of the stitch is worked over 1,2,3,4 intersections of canvas and then repeated, forming arrowheads. In the second stage of working, stitches over two intersections are placed against the three shorter stitches of the original line. Then the arrowheads are repeated, pointing the opposite way. Note that the longest stitches form a line diagonally across the canvas, unlike Milanese where long and short stitches alternate.

Parisian

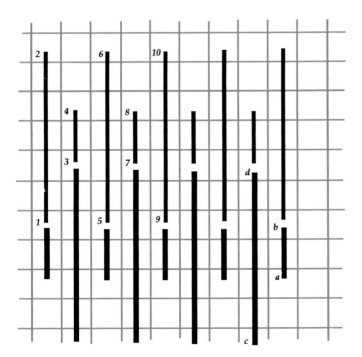

Parisian is a useful and simply worked straight stitch in which stitches over two and six horizontal threads alternate. On the second row the long stitch is worked against the short and vice versa. As with all straight stitches, Parisian may be worked sideways. A small version may be worked over three and one threads.

This is one of twelve watercolours used for a calendar, and is of a type which particularly lends itself to a tonal treatment such as the one opposite. The house with its surroundings has fairly simple outlines and is not dependent on colour for its charm.

Cottage in sepia tones

This delightful small picture was produced by a student of the author during a five-day course. It was drawn from imagination and was the first attempt at needlepoint by this student. This picture is worked in crewel wools on 13s interlock canvas.

Stitches used:

Sky: Single brick stitch.

Roof: Brick stitch.

Chimney: Small Parisian worked sideways with French knots for smoke.

House walls: Brickwork stitch worked sideways.

Window frames: Outlined in tent stitch and straight stitches with straight stitch glazing bars.

Windows: Tent stitch.

Door: Tent stitch.

Trees on left: Chevron stitch in two shades and mosaic stitch.

Tree on right: Tent stitch with French knot flowers.

Fencing: Single trammed Gobelin and tent stitch.

Bushes: French knots and random straight stitches.

Satin

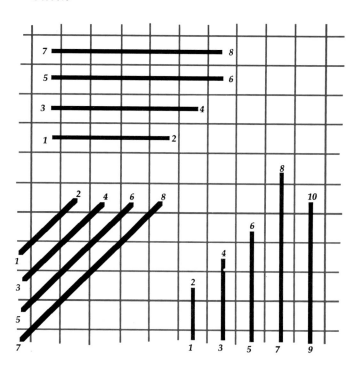

Satin stitches are parallel stitches worked either straight or diagonally on the canvas. For a smooth, neat effect the tension must be kept firm and even, and the stitches worked in an 'over and over' fashion.

Spider's web

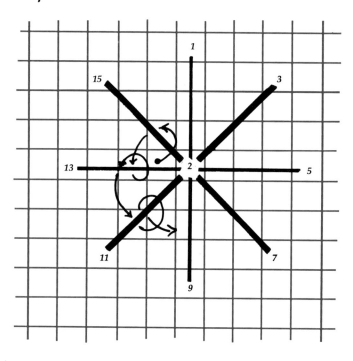

For this three-dimensional stitch a basic star shape with eight legs into the central hole must first be firmly laid down. Next bring the needle and thread to the surface of the canvas between any two legs of the star, then take the needle back over one leg and forward under two legs, without going through to the back of the canvas. Keep the centre hole towards you as you work and keep turning the canvas if possible. Pull the stitches gently along the leg towards the centre so that a firm, hard stitch is made. When the web is completely filled take the needle to the back and fasten off.

Split

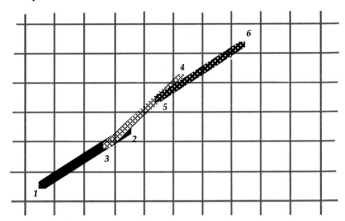

As its name implies, in split stitch the second and following stitches are worked through the preceding stitch, splitting the thread as nearly as possible through the centre. Split stitch may be worked at any angle across the canvas.

Stem

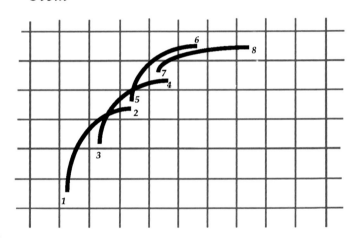

Stem stitch may be worked in any direction across the canvas, the beginning of each stitch being about half way along the preceding stitch, either underneath it or above it, depending on which way the line of stitchery is to be taken.

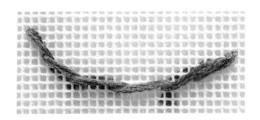

Tent, basketweave

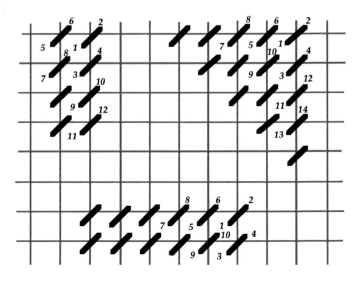

Basketweave tent stitch is worked in diagonal lines up and down the canvas, each stitch being over one intersection of the canvas. Worked in this way, the tensions of the stitch remain even and there is no distortion of the canvas. Avoid working two lines of stitchery in the same direction (which results in the surface being less smooth). Stop work for a rest in the middle of a row rather than at the end, as otherwise it is difficult to tell which way you worked the last row.

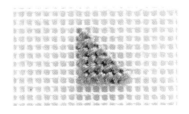

Tent, continental

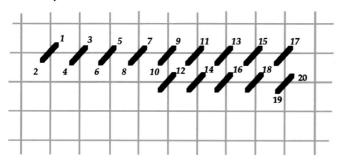

Follow the numbering on the diagram carefully to ensure that each row is made in the same way: each stitch is made from right to left when the row is worked from left to right, and vice versa. Continental tent stitch will distort the canvas if more than a small area is covered.

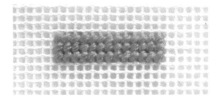

Twill

Double Twill

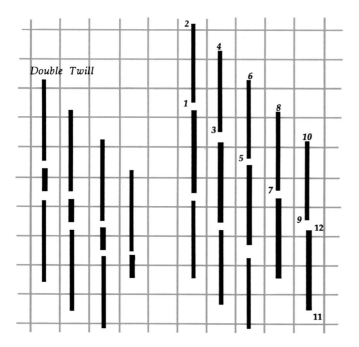

Twill is an effective, easily worked straight stitch which has the appearance of a diagonal stitch on the canvas. Straight stitches, usually over three or four horizontal canvas threads, are worked stepping down the canvas one thread with each stitch. Work the second row up the diagonal as shown on the diagram. Double twill is the same except that alternate rows are worked over one or two threads of canvas.

Water

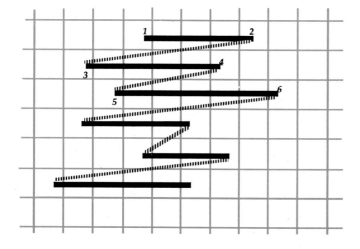

By working random straight stitches in the manner shown on the diagram, the canvas may be covered without splitting any of the threads. It is also possible to use many different colour shadings in this stitch, which very useful if the subject is, indeed, water.

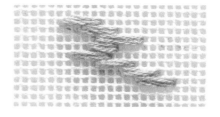

Waterfall

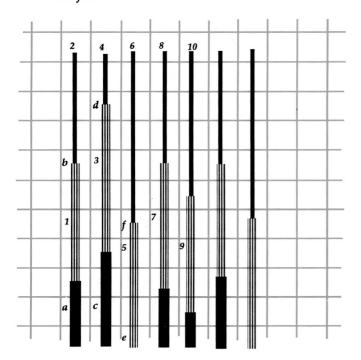

Waterfall stitch was developed to give a smooth interwoven but random effect, and as such has many uses. Firstly lines of random straight stitches are worked and then the stitches below are usually worked into them, splitting the threads, or less often between them. The figures and letters on the diagram indicate the start of the stitch even if hidden by a subsequent stitch.

Woven plait

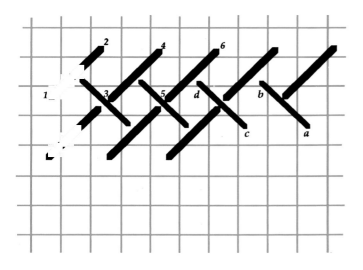

The interwoven basketweave effect formed by this stitch is unlike any other and as such can form a good contrast. It is easily worked, though fairly time-consuming. One row of diagonal stitches is worked at a time and the top of the stitch on the following row is made into the hole which is nearly masked by the stitch of the preceding row.

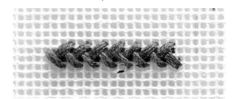

6 Alphabets and Numerals

You may feel, when you have finished working your house, that you would like to give it a stitched title and date. If nothing else, you should certainly sign your work in some way, even if it is only a set of stitched initials worked in surface stitchery in a corner. Think how interesting it is for us to look at old samplers and notice when they were embroidered and by whom. There are many books which deal exclusively with samplers, and two of these have been included in the bibliography, so that you can, if you wish, look more deeply into the subject of lettering for embroidery. Such old samplers were usually worked on fine evenweave linens, therefore no background stitchery around the lettering was needed, as threads taken across the back of the work did not show through on the front. When working on canvas, however, even such a fine canvas as 18s, strands of thread taken across the back of the bare canvas between letters or numbers will show through when viewed from the front. It *is* possible to work each letter individually and finish off all the ends very neatly so that nothing is visible from the front except the lettering, but this is difficult to achieve, and you will probably find it easier to fill in all the background round the lettering with basketweave tent stitch.

In this chapter are included four alphabets and three sets of numerals. They are different sizes and styles and are suitable for use in a panel or border under the picture of your house. They can be worked in either tent or single cross stitch. Cross stitch, being symmetrical, gives a more finished look to the letters, but tent is less time consuming. A title may be worked on a finer mesh canvas than the main work, so that the lettering is small, and then this panel can be appliquéd on to the main piece of canvas or let into the mount if the picture is being framed.

If you just want to insert a set of initials unobtrusively in the corner of your picture, it is best to use a tiny chain or back stitch in a fine thread as surface stitchery on a smooth part of the work. If you are working directly on to the canvas the positioning of the letters should be worked out carefully on squared paper before you begin stitching, as it is very easy to make mistakes with spacing the letters if you do not do any preparatory work.

The alphabets may be used singly, that is, all upper case (capital letters), or all lower case (small letters), or used with capitals at the beginning of some or all of the words. The letters in Alphabet 4 are particularly suitable for initials, but may be used as capitals with the lower case letters of Alphabet 1. Alphabet 2 is a more modern lower case alphabet and would look well with the capitals of Alphabet 3.

The numbers in Numerals 1 are suitable for use with Alphabets 1 and 4 as they are the same height. The numbers in Numerals 2 are the same height as Alphabets 2 and 3. The Roman numerals are smaller than either of the other two, but could easily be extended if required.

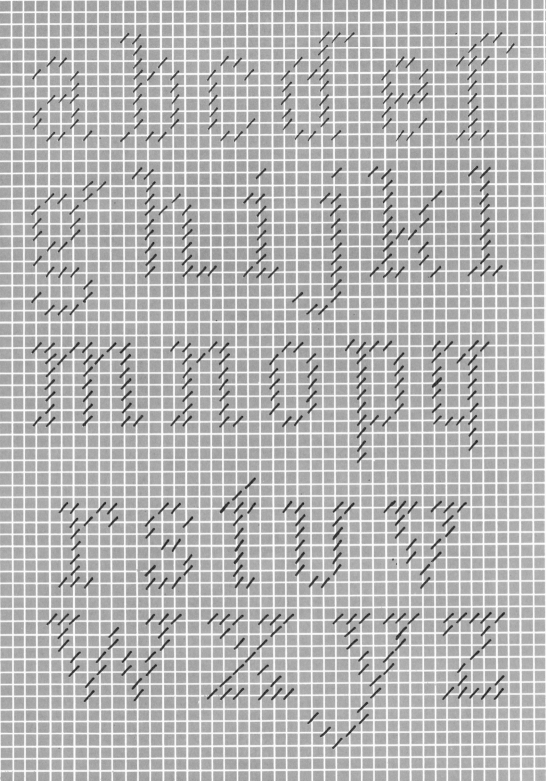

Alphabet 1

Bruges – stitches used:

Sky: Twill stitch.

Roof: An interlocking satin stitch motif over 1,2,4,6,4,2 canvas threads. The tops of the stitches over 4,6,4 threads are at the same level.

House walls: Upright cross stitch.

Window frames and surrounds: Tent stitch.

Windows: Tent stitch with glazing bars added as surface stitchery using one strand of 6-strand embroidery floss.

Doors: Double rows of cross stitches.

Drainpipes: Single strands of thread across the surface of the upright cross stitch walls.

Base of the building: A line of diagonal satin stitch over two threads of canvas.

Grass in foreground: Arrowhead stitch in two shades of green with groups of French knots.

Trees on right: From the top: leaf stitch, mosaic stitch with French knots, single trammed Gobelin with self-coloured French knots.

Trees on left: From the top: fly stitch, massed French knots, jacquard stitch in three colours with added French knots.

Bush on right: Bullion stitch in green and blue.

Bruges

This is the type of formal picture which may be worked following a memorable holiday. It was copied from a small coloured drawing in a travel agent's brochure, the original picture being enlarged to the size required on a photocopier. The main features were then traced through on to the canvas. As this was not a picture of a known scene, the trees and bushes surrounding the terrace of houses were changed in shape to suit a variety of decorative stitches. The title, in the two languages used in Belgium, was carefully worked, letter by letter, without any background stitchery, and was made so that it could be let into the mount when the picture was framed. This picture is worked in 6-strand embroidery floss on 18s interlock canvas.

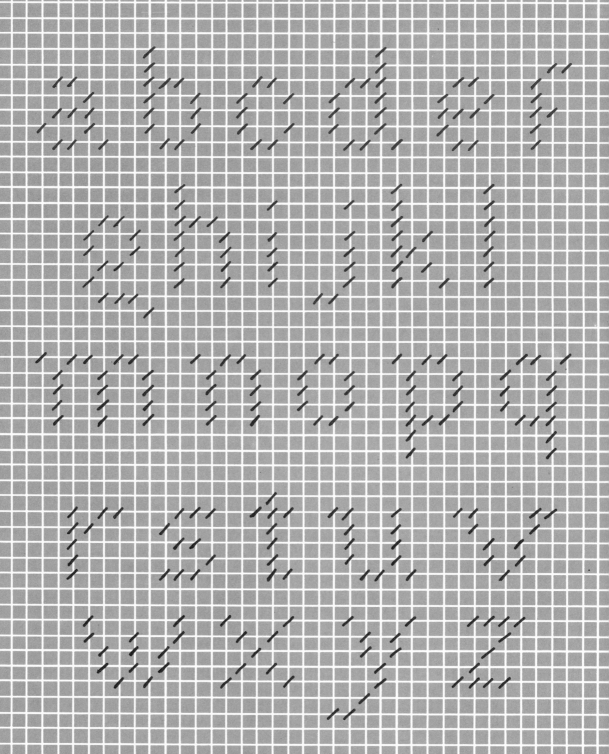

Alphabet 2

Alphabet 3

Decorative Brick House – stitches used:

Sky: Diagonal mosaic stitch.

Roof: Single brick stitch worked sideways. A single long stitch runs along the bottom of the roof in the same colour mixture, of dark grey and deep mauve, as the roof.

Chimney: Single brick stitch round single cross stitch patterns. Deep mauve chimney pots.

House walls: Brickwork stitch in a mixture of two shades of honey gold with patterns in single cross stitch and tent stitch. Horizontal divisions of the walls in single trammed Gobelin stitch.

Window frames: Tent stitch, as are the glazing bars.

Windows: Diagonal satin stitch worked in a mixture of grey and white.

Door: Tent stitch and diagonal satin stitch, worked in dark colours to suggest the fact that it is set well back inside the porchway.

Porch: Tent stitch uprights with back stitch arch. Arches are difficult to portray on a small scale; several rows of back stitch following the exact line of the arch are usually the best way of showing them.

Garden wall: Brick stitch in two shades of brown.

Paths: Staggered diagonal satin stitch blocks.

Decorative Brick House

A house like this might have been designed especially to be copied as a needlepoint picture! The intricate brickwork in its different colours can be copied almost exactly on to the canvas mesh. Terraces of small brick houses were a common feature of the late Victorian age in Britain, but not many were as decorative as this one in South Wales. The balcony has been omitted as it was thought it would spoil the effect of the line of decoration above the bay window. The curtains have also been left out as it seemed possible they might detract from the main features of the house. This picture is worked in 6-strand embroidery floss on 18s interlock canvas.

Alphabet 4

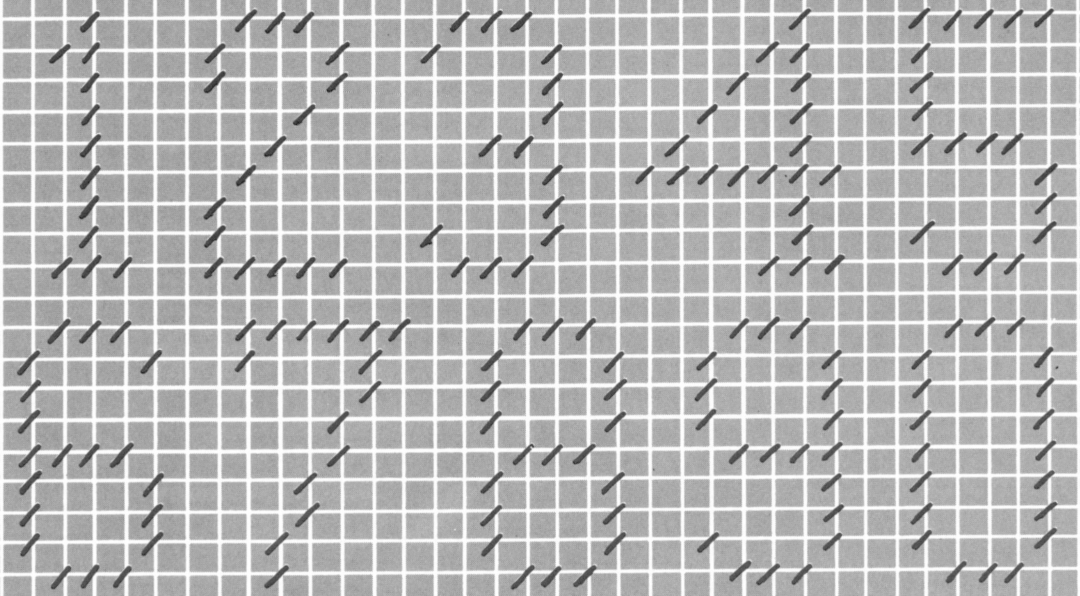

Numerals 1

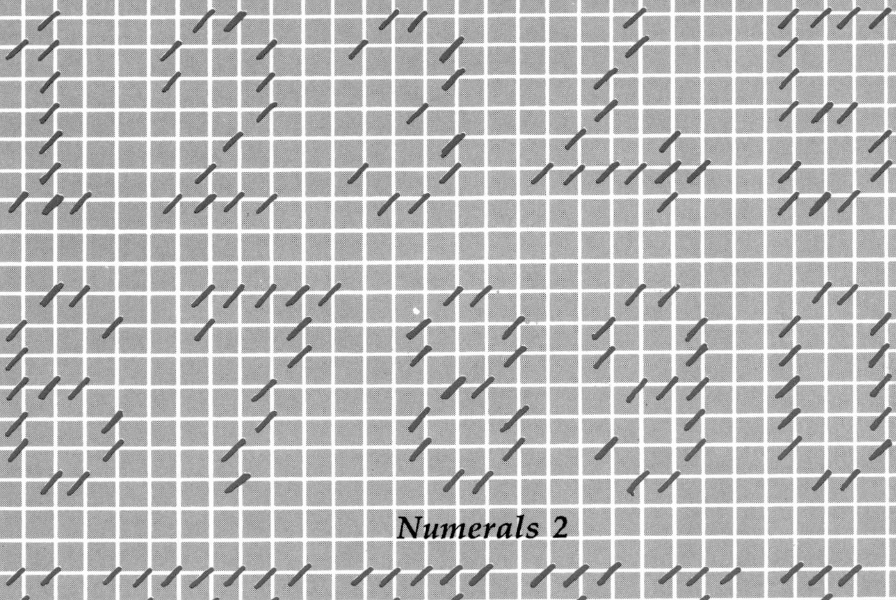

Numerals 2

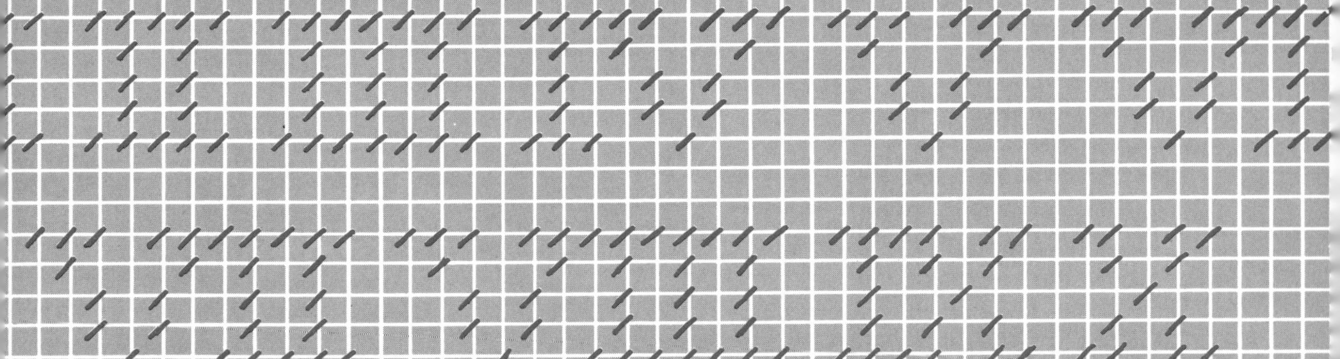

Numerals 3

New Zealand Waterfront Houses– stitches used:

Roofs: The green and the mauve roofs are single trammed Gobelin. The gables of the cream-coloured houses are outlined in split stitch and filled with Gobelin stitch, while the split stitch outline of the pink roof is filled with one line of Gobelin stitch and three straight stitches each held down by a stitch across the middle.

House walls: Gobelin stitch of varying widths to represent weatherboarding.

Window frames: Tent stitch, as are the glazing bars.

Windows: Diagonal satin stitch worked in black.

Shop front: Gobelin stitch in black.

Walls: The top wall is single brick stitch worked sideways, while the lower wall is brick stitch worked sideways. The steps are single trammed Gobelin.

Boathouses: Horizontal satin stitch blocks form the doors and gables and sloping satin stitch is used for the front walls.

Boats: Waterfall stitch worked sideways.

Water: Water stitch in a mixture of blues, grey and turquoises.

Sea wall: Double brick stitch in a mixture of black and dark green.

Wooded background: Random Florentine stitch in a mixture of dark greens.

New Zealand Waterfront Houses

These are very different sorts of houses from those found in Europe, being constructed of different types of weatherboarding, but in their varying colours and the way in which they vye with each other for views of the harbour, they make a most attractive scene. The original picture was much cluttered with overhead wires, rigging on the boats, washing lines and other everyday items which have been omitted on this picture. This picture is worked in crewel wools on 13s interlock canvas.

7 Stretching and Finishing

When you have finished working your house in needlepoint, do not be disappointed if the general effect is rather crumpled and parts of the canvas are decidedly out of shape. The stretching and finishing processes are necessary to achieve the very best final result, and must be carried out carefully.

First you should gather together the items you will need:

1. A piece of plywood or fibreboard larger than the work to be stretched. On this should be stuck a sheet of paper marked out with either the exact size the work should measure, or several lines about half an inch (1cm) apart, drawn parallel to the edges of the work, so that they may be seen through the canvas mesh. A piece of clear polythene should be stuck or stapled down over this paper.
2. A staple gun for use on plywood, or small tacks for use on fibreboard.
3. Starch wallpaper paste with a small bowl for mixing.
4. Round-ended knife for spreading.
5. Clean damp cloth.
6. Small piece of thin towelling.

Proceed as follows:

Carefully dampen the *back* of the picture with the cloth. Some pictures hardly need to be dampened at all, as they are not out of shape to any degree. If a large area has been worked in a diagonal stitch, however, this part may have to be dampened more than the rest of the work, to enable you to pull it gently back to its correct proportions.

Lay the picture face down on the board. If a lot of three-dimensional stitches have been used, put a piece of thin towelling the same size as the worked area underneath the picture so that the stitches do not get squashed.

Line up a set of holes in your canvas, about a quarter of an inch (0.5cm) away from the bottom edge of the work, with one of the lines marked on your board. If you have the exact size of the picture marked out, begin by lining up the bottom of your needlepoint with the bottom line of your outline. Staple or tack this edge down, pulling it to the correct length. Work round the picture, one side at a time, lining up the work with appropriate lines on the board, until the whole picture is firmly held down and measures the correct size. You may have to go back and make some adjustments to various parts.

Now mix a small quantity of paste to a soft, fluffy consistency and apply a thin layer gently but fairly firmly to the back of the stitched area only. You may work this into the threads on the back in the areas where there is a good covering, but be very circumspect in the parts where the stitches have little backing, such as brickwork stitch, as otherwise the paste may seep through on to the front of the work. Leave to dry naturally.

If, when you take the picture off the board, you find one or two features are not quite straight, it is possible to dampen the wallpaper paste again and soften as much of it as is necessary to enable you to pull the offending area straight. Pin the picture out on the board in the same way as before, but face up this time so that you can see exactly what you are doing. Leave to dry as before.

Place the canvas face down
on the board, with a piece
of towelling underneath the
stitched area only, if three-
dimensional stitches have
been used.

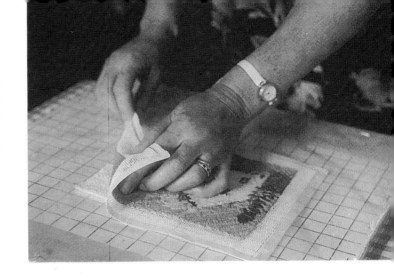

Staple or tack the canvas to
the board, pulling the
picture to the correct size
and aligning the edges
along the parallel lines on
the board.

Apply a thin layer of paste
to the back of the stitched
area only, being careful to
avoid too much pressure on
areas where the stitches
have little backing.

Bibliography

Christensen, Jo Ippolito *The Needlepoint Book,*
New York 1986

Don, Sarah *Traditional Samplers,* London 1986

Enthoven, Jacqueline *Stitches with Variations,*
California, 1985

Good Housekeeping *Needlepoint,* London 1981

Gray, Jennifer *Canvas Work,* London 1955

Hanley, Hope *101 Needlepoint Stitches & how to
use them,* New York 1986

Hanley, Hope *Needlepoint,* New York 1964

Higginson, Susan *Needlepoint Miniatures,*
London 1987

Higginson, Susan *The Book of Needlepoint
Stitches,* London 1989

Kay, Dorothea, *Sew a Sampler,* London 1979

Messent, Jan *Embroidery & Architecture,*
London 1985

Pearson, Anna *First Steps in Needlepoint,*
London 1985

Windrum, Sarah *Needlepoint,* London 1982

Suppliers

UNITED KINGDOM
The Royal School of Needlework Mail Order
Little Barrington
Burford
OXFORD OX8 4TE

WHI Tapestry Shop
84 Pimlico Road
LONDON SW1

Mace and Nairn
89 Crane Street
SALISBURY
Wilts SP1 2PY

The Embroidery Shop
51 William Street
EDINBURGH EH3 7LW

U.S.A.
American Crewel and Canvas
P.O. Box 453
CANASTOTA
NY 13032

AUSTRALIA
Penguin Threads Pty Ltd
25-27 Izett Street
PRAHAN 3181
Victoria

Index